GOD'S FOREVER WORD

by Jeff Farnham

Post Office Box 1099 • Murfreesboro, Tennessee 37133
(800) 251-4100 • (615) 893-6700 • FAX (615) 848-6943
swordofthelord.com

DEDICATION

To my lovely bride and wife Kathryn

A worshiper of God in spirit and in truth

A zealous, faithful student of God's Word

A fervent laborer in prayer and intercession

A selfless lover to me, her grateful husband

A compassionate heart in our Christian home

A devoted encourager to our five children

A glorious crown to our ministry

TABLE ⬤F

pg. vi   Preface

pg.viii   Introduction

pg. 1   Let Me Introduce You to the Author   **1**

pg. 9   The Testimony of the Author About His Book   **2**

pg. 25   Let Me Introduce You to the Problem   **3**

pg. 37   An Enemy Hath Done This   **4**

pg. 59   Nonpreservation and the Impotence of God   **5**

pg. 69   Does Translation Contaminate?   **6**

pg. 79   That It Might Be Fulfilled Which Was Spoken   **7**

C●NTENTS

8   English Bible for an English-Speaking People   *pg. 87*

9   English Words for an English-Speaking People   *pg. 95*

10   English Grammar for an English-Speaking People   *pg. 105*

11   The New International Shakespeare
and the New American Standard Chaucer   *pg. 111*

12   Truth: Absolute or Approximate?   *pg. 121*

13   Emmaus Road Doctorates   *pg. 133*

14   The Long and the Short of It   *pg. 155*

15   What's It Really All About?   *pg. 161*

GLOSSARY *pg.165*

PREFACE

Modern students of bibliology have at their disposal an increasingly large number of solidly Baptist, philosophically fundamental publications that will profit them in understanding the all-important truth of the inspiration and preservation of Scripture in the King James Version of the Bible for the English-speaking world. This writing is not an effort to outshine or correct other similar endeavors, for indeed many of the other books possess strong scholarship, and many of the various authors have conducted extensive research.

Rather, I have undertaken to write this book to enhance the others and to complement them. May the Lord who does uphold His Word in all generations use this and other works penned by God-fearing writers to show you that through inspiration and preservation, the Scripture of the faithful King James translation is indeed reliable, infallible, perfect, and profitable in the English language for the twenty-first century and forever.

INTRODUCTION

Ours is a day and age of doubt, unbelief, and flat-out rejection of absolute truth in the sphere of biblical revelation. This is hardly a surprise. A brief look at history shows cyclic periods in which the Bible has undergone attack. It has been banned, barred, belittled, bickered about, blasted, burned, and by-passed; but thanks be to God, "the word of God is not bound" (II Timothy 2:9), and "the scripture cannot be broken" (John 10:35). Beyond the record of history is the biblical explanation for it all: "For the time will come when they will not endure sound doctrine...And they shall turn away their ears from the truth" (II Timothy 4:3, 4).

In the specific context of our day, the Word of God is being attacked through employment of the most insidious of all wiles and tactics. The Bible-haters of the last century contrived a clever and enticing combination of perversion and merchandising that has left the entire general public and much of the churched public of this day without the pure truth. The battle for the truth of God relates directly to the issue of *one preserved version* versus *myriad perverted versions*.

Much of the contention in fundamental circles today regarding the King James Version is due, in part, to reliance upon human research in drawing conclusions. For all that a scholar can find on the subjects of inspiration and preservation, he will never enter into the realms of truth if he does not find his answers in God's Word. To address the inspiration-preservation issue through use of man's intellect leaves the student of Scripture dangling from the outmost limbs of doubt and insecurity.

If one is to address this issue in honesty, he must ask, "Who is God, and what does He say about His Scripture?"

Herein lie the two greatest needs for the student of Scripture. **First,** he must approach the issue of scriptural veracity in light of the miraculous, not in light of the mundane. No other book in all of created time has been authored by the Holy Ghost. Therefore, to study its contents as if it were a physics text is useless! It is absurd to think that the Holy Ghost has authored a book and then left it up to men to preserve it, much less to question its preservation! God can authoritatively speak of inspiration and preservation, and He has adequately done so. He has every right to do so. No man has the right to impugn the character of God by harboring one single doubt on this matter!

Second, he must approach the issue of scriptural veracity upon the basis of faith, not upon the basis of intellect. This is a restatement of the general theme of I Corinthians, chapter 1: God's wisdom versus man's. To engage oneself in the study of God's Word "to find the variants and mistakes" is to disregard faith immediately and to disassemble faith ultimately. Scholarship must bow before and submit to faith before the first verse of Scripture is ever read; otherwise, the whole study will rot from the inside out.

Everything you add to the truth subtracts from the truth.
—Chinese proverb

"He who sets his own copy keeps writing worse and worse."
—Frances E. Willard

The crowd that will not accept one truth will decay to the point that is does not accept one God: many denominations, many translations, many gods.

"We must not covet to be wise above that which God has written for us."— Matthew Henry

Inspiration without preservation is a worthless doctrine.

1

Let Me Introduce You to the Author

When it comes to the issues of bibliology facing the present-day believer, one of the main issues is that of authorship. The multiplicity of occurrences of "Thus saith the Lord," "For the Lord hath spoken," "As it is written," and other related wordings in the Word of God give the reader unambiguous guidance to the only possible conclusion regarding authorship: God Himself. In the person of the Holy Spirit, also named the Holy Ghost, the third Person in the Godhead, God chose and then authorized every specific word of His truth.

The impeccable perfections of God's character dictate that the Bible He gave would be equally flawless. Indeed, if God could say something that would be false in any way, then not only His integrity and trustworthiness, but also His revelation, would be suspect. Thankfully, no suspicion is warranted. When Moses asked God to show him His way and His glory, God responded by hiding His beloved servant in a cleft of the rock. As the Lord passed, He removed His hand such that Moses could see God's "back parts," not His face; for seeing God's face would have killed Moses. In that grand display, "the Lord passed by before him, and proclaimed, The Lord, the Lord God, merciful and gracious, longsuffering, and abundant in goodness and truth" (Exodus 34:6). Later, in giving his final words to the Israelites, Moses exalted the name of Jehovah God and said, "He is the Rock, his work is perfect: for all his ways are judgment: a God of truth and without iniquity, just and right is he" (Deuteronomy 32:4).

David, writing in the wilderness of Ziph between Saul's relentless efforts to capture him, confessed, "Into thine hand I commit my spirit: thou hast redeemed me, O Lord God of truth" (Psalm 31:5). Immediately following the close call with Saul's men in Engedi, he declared "God shall send forth his mercy and his truth" (57:3). At the very end of his life, as he was transferring the kingdom to Solomon and charging him with regard to the building of the temple and reigning over the people of Israel, David informed the congregation assembled for the occasion, "But thou, O Lord, art a God full of compassion, and gracious, longsuffering, and plenteous in mercy and truth" (86:15).

The prophets attested to God's truthfulness and trustworthiness as well. Isaiah said, "Thy counsels of old are faithfulness and truth" (Isaiah 25:1). Twice in Isaiah 65:16, that great patrician prophet referenced the Lord as the God of truth.

Paul referred three times to the truth of God (Romans 1:25; 3:7; and 15:8). Because He is the God of truth, man has the privilege of hearing and knowing the truth of God. His truthfulness and His truth are undeniably inseparable from each other and from Him. His truthfulness is the wellspring from which His truth flows.

All the bickering and bantering about men and their role in "corrupting" the Word of God has overlooked and excluded the unique and incomparable Author Himself! God is made very little in these discussions about presumably necessary errors in the Bible, while man is made very big. A similar debacle is the ongoing discussions and symposiums about global warming. Supposedly man is big enough to interrupt the environment and initiate cataclysms as if God cannot keep his earth! God promised Noah that "while the earth remaineth, seedtime and harvest, and cold and heat, and summer and winter, and day and night shall not cease" (Genesis 8:22). God is still big enough to manage the world He spoke into existence ex nihilo! So bah, humbug on global warming!

And bah, humbug to the fourth degree on a mentality of bibliology that relegates God to such a small and insignificant role that He cannot oversee the preservation of His truth through the introduction of new languages, the translations from one language to another, and the changes within all those languages. Indeed, for the generations of man who have come after the recipients of the original autographa to have

2

the truth of God from the God of truth, He must have preserved it!

Mistake-theorists who insist that Scripture has not been perfectly preserved through centuries of time, and therefore that the King James Version is not flawlessly preserved, are either inadvertently or purposely shaming the Author of the Authorized Version. These perversion pundits do not pretend to tell us when the perversion and mistakes came about because that would require them to define which generations had the truth and which ones did not. Such a position, of necessity, dictates that its proponents identify a specific time in history before which Scripture was inerrant and after which it was flawed. Did this happen in the second century A.D.? the fifth? how about the tenth or sixteenth? When did this error-laden Scripture supercede the unflawed version and plunge mankind into the abyss of having from then on an imperfect Bible? From then on, that is, until the pseudo-scholars of the late twentieth and early twenty-first centuries could inform us and bring about the evolution of the oldest known manuscripts to create the true Word of God.

Logically, without divine preservation, the inspired integrity of God's Word disintegrated immediately after the generation of original recipients. What must be concluded is that no generation since A.D.100 has ever had any portion of the inspired Word of God. If no generation after that time had the perfect Word of God, then all who preach Jesus Christ crucified, risen and coming again are vain preachers to vain hearers, false witnesses of fake hopes, and most miserable of men among the most sinful of men!

One Author, Many Contributors. The singular Author of Scripture must be distinguished from the multiple writers of Scripture. Approximately forty "holy men of God spake as they were moved by the Holy Ghost" (II Peter 1:21) and thus became contributing writers of the dictated words of God, but they were by no means the authors of the Word of God. God is the Author, solely and singularly responsible for each word which He chose specifically for the purpose of communicating to mankind.

Contributors to Scripture in the Old Testament range from men whose writing ministry is clearly known and widely accepted among Christian conservatives to men whose possible contribution to the

3

sixty-six books of the canon is either questionable or unknown. The list of certain Old Testament writers of Scripture begins with Job and Moses, and in a generally agreed upon chronology includes Joshua, Samuel, David, Ethan, Solomon, Asaph, Obadiah, Joel, Jonah, Amos, Hosea, Isaiah, Micah, Nahum, Zephaniah, Habakkuk, Jeremiah, Daniel, Ezekiel, Haggai, Zechariah, Ezra, Mordecai, Nehemiah, and Malachi. Other Old Testament writers include Boaz who possibly wrote Judges and Ruth; Elijah, Elisha or Nathan who possibly wrote I and II Kings; Hezekiah who possibly wrote some Psalms; and Zorobabel who possibly wrote some of the restoration Psalms.

New Testament writers include the four penmen of the Gospels Matthew, Mark, Luke, and John along with the epistle writers Paul, Peter, James, and Jude.

Gloriously sanctified though they were, all those writers were but holy men of God. Highly called, each one was consecrated to unique service in writing Scripture; however, each one was desecrated by a sin nature because each one was a man. None of them could have possibly written even one book of Scripture without having errors. Each one was prone to his own sins and faults and failures. Job had his misunderstanding, and Moses had his anger. David had his adultery, and Solomon had his carnality. John had his eye on elevated position in the kingdom. Peter had his heart in the wrong place at the crucifixion. However, when God superintended the writing of His Word, each of these approximately forty men was for that moment and time transformed and purged into "a vessel unto honour, sanctified, and meet for the master's use, and prepared unto every good work" (II Timothy 2:21).

One Author, No Collusion. This Author is the God who never engages in collusion. The many contributors to Scripture did not secretly aspire to define and declare God as they saw Him. They wrote in cooperation with God, not in collusion with each other. One of God's purposes in using men to write Scripture over a period of two thousand years was to make it impossible for them to collude in any effort to make their own revelation.

In essence, liberals and compromisers are developing a Bible in much the same way that scientists claim the world and all its creatures and matter developed. Supposedly educated minds who are attempting

4

to convince mankind of evolutionary origination are superceded in their sin only by those attempting to persuade mankind of erroneous revelation. Creation demands a Creator, but evolution demands only a mysterious "big bang" followed by an unattended process of random development. Inspiration and preservation demand an authorizing Preserver; however, the multiversion approach requires only that there be a "big bang" of inspiration—with the word inspiration subject to arbitrary definition—followed by a designless combination of events that has allowed the Scripture to progress with variations and mutations, much as evolutionsts say the animal kingdom has developed.

Today's Westcott-Hort theorists, multiversionists, and Bible correctors are scheming to bring a reliable Bible up out of the imperfect morass of tainted and tampered manuscripts. What is this, if it is not the evolution of the Bible, a collusion of the intellectually elite with the financially astute to deceive the spiritually inept?

One Author, No Contradiction. This Author is the God who does not contradict Himself, for "it [is] impossible for God to lie" (Hebrews 6:18), and He is the "God, that cannot lie" (Titus 1:2). In any given contradiction, at least one position is a lie. Nowhere in all of God's Word is there a proven contradiction; furthermore, any apparent contradictions are easily reconciled when full attention is given to parallel passages, context and other hermeneutical factors.

With regard to the inspiration-preservation debate, perhaps no more chilling statement can be quoted than "Professing themselves to be wise, they became fools...Who changed the truth of God into a lie" (Romans 1:22, 25). While the second part of that quotation is not from the same sentence as the first part, the progression of Romans chapter one is from a self-profession of wisdom that is really foolishness to a changing of God's truth into a lie. When higher critics place extant and variant manuscripts on a par with the Majority Text, the result is that those supposedly wise individuals become fools by a process that essentially makes God a liar. Any position that claims that Scripture contains translators' errors or copyists' oversights must ultimately claim that God's truth has become untrue in places. That changes the truth of God into a lie.

Another of God's commentaries on the role of men in the realm of higher criticism is, "Yea, let God be true, but every man a liar" (3:4). Every man who aspires to prove that the King James Bible is a flawed English edition—indeed just another of many reasonable efforts at translation—must grapple with this arresting thought. God is true. Any man who would support the concept that God could be anything but true in His revelation to man is a liar. Higher criticism has brought to us a multiplicity of contradictory records, and the higher critics are seeking to convince the general public that a non-contradictory Scripture can develop from contradictory manuscripts. God's writers engaged in no collusion, but this work of higher criticism is collusion. God cannot contradict Himself, but in this higher criticism is contradiction.

One Author, No Corruption. This author is the God who does not corrupt Himself. The issue of inspiration may find common ground concerning the original autographa, except among the outright infidels and apostates. Most will agree that God inspired the exact prophecies to the prophets and epistles to the apostles. However, the issue of preservation is the source of much contention. The scoffers dare to believe that what God gave in perfection He has allowed to fall into corruption. The prevailing winds of deterioration of the supernatural and exaltation of the natural find the doctrine of preservation troubling. The impeccable character of Scripture's Author is impugned by claims that the Bible has fallen into disrepair through translations and language changes.

Again, it must be asserted that God is incorruptible; therefore, His Word must also be incorruptible. In the days of Samuel, after years when "the word of the Lord was precious [and] there was no open vision" (I Samuel 3:1), "the Lord appeared again in Shiloh: for the Lord revealed himself to Samuel in Shiloh by the word of the Lord" (3:21). Commenting on this, the Holy Ghost said, "And Samuel grew, and the Lord was with him, and did let none of his words fall to the ground" (3:19). That God was not speaking of Samuel's own words not falling to the ground is clear because "we must needs die, and are as water spilt on the ground, which cannot be gathered up again" (II Samuel 14:14). Obviously, God was referencing His own words in and through Samuel. It is conclusive that nothing God said to Samuel and subsequently through him corrupted. Nor has there been any corruption of anything God ever said through inspiration to His human writers, because He has preserved it all.

One Author, No Confusion. This Author is the God who does not confuse Himself. Any failure of the exact work of preservation superintended by the Holy Ghost would constitute a confusion. Once perfection has been assumed irrelevant, the entire Scripture becomes suspect, and the result is confusion as to what is truth and what is not. God is the God of light for the pathway, not darkness. He gives truth, not lies. He speaks hope, not despair. There is neither light nor truth nor hope in the "doubtful disputations" (Romans 14:1) of the non-preservationists because the very promises of the Author that give light and truth and hope are deemed unreliable! There is neither light nor truth nor hope in the "fables…which minister questions, rather than godly edifying which is in faith" (I Timothy 1:4). The confusing questions as to the veracity and infallibility of the very words of God have produced a darkened, deceived, despairing generation because the very people who listen to the confusion must, of necessity, dwell without light, truth and hope.

One Author, No Confinement. This author is the God who does not confine Himself. While man is, of necessity through his finiteness, confined to limitations; God the Author, of merit due to His infiniteness, is not confined at all. At His prerogative, God may quote exactly in the New Testament from the Old. Just as surely, he may alter an Old Testament wording for its placement in the New. This change by the Author is acceptable because He is perfect, infinite and flawless. He has the right through progressive revelation to add information in the New Testament that was withheld in the Old. He has the right through focus of application to omit information found in an Old Testament passage for its usage in the New. He has the right through purpose of communication to transcend the ages and relate a truth in one age via different words than He used in a previous age and still aver, "It is written." Why? Because he is the infinite, divine, perfect, truthful Author.

Perhaps more than any other issue, the actual identity of the Author of Scripture is the most important. The wiser and bigger the God of the Bible is in the mind of any particular individual, the easier it is for that person to accept divine preservation. The more any person receives the infinite righteousness and holiness of God, the less difficulty he has in believing in Scripture preservation. The more miraculous and infinite the Godhead becomes in the apprehension of any particular soul, the less trouble that one will encounter in shouting Amen! to Scripture preservation.

Only those who believe God to be God as man reveals God will find themselves in any quandary as to the veracity and accuracy of the King James Version of the Holy Scriptures for the English-speaking world.

All in all, anyone who will believe God to be God as God reveals God will never be troubled about the impeccability and immutability and infallibility of the Word of God. God authored it for all generations, and he is well able to keep it for them.

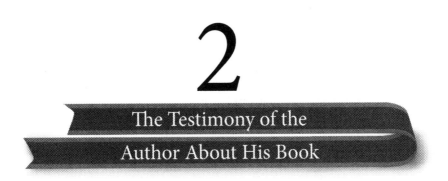

2

The Testimony of the
Author About His Book

No one is more an authority about any book than the author of that book. If readers puzzle over nuances and innuendo found within a text, their best resource to find answers to their dilemmas is direct contact with the author. The author is the expert on the original intent of his statements, the contextual development of his work, and the breadth and depth of applications of any thing he has written. He is the "go-to" person for any question concerning whether a portion is literal or figurative. That author can answer any confusion regarding any unclear matter within his own publication.

God, the attested and agreed upon Author of Scripture, has clearly told His readers plenty about His Book, the Bible. He did not leave Himself without witness; nor did He leave His readers bereft of testimony with regard to what He said, why He said it, or to whom He said it. Quite evident within the paragraphs and pages of the Holy Scripture is a running commentary from the Author Himself about His magnum opus. Careful readers will easily see this glorious strain of information. Casual readers will but stumble across a tidbit here and there and perhaps wonder what it is about. Careless readers will miss it altogether. Even still, the commentary is there, and this chapter is a humble attempt to at least touch the hem of the garment on the subject of what the Author said about the book He authorized holy men to write.

The External Testimony of God About His Book. The Word of God speaks of events which later occurred outside the realm of Scripture itself. The specificity with which those events match the Bible's record prove the divine origin and preservation of the Word of God. No work of man could ever come close to the perfection that one finds in God's Book with regard to these matters.

The Alteration in Wicked Hearts. The heart of any man is certainly external to the Scripture itself. That heart—described by Jeremiah as "deceitful above all things, and desperately wicked" (Jeremiah 17:9); cited by the Lord Jesus Christ Himself as the source of "evil thoughts, murders, adulteries, fornications, thefts, false witness, [and] blasphemies" (Matthew 15:19); declared by Paul to be "darkened," "hard[ened,] and impenitent," (Romans 1:21; 2:5); criticized by James as capable of self-deception (James 1:26); described by Peter as "exercised with covetous practices" (II Peter 2:14); and referenced by John as possessing the inherent power to "condemn us" from within (I John 3:20)—was created by the same Creator God as the one who authored the Scriptures. However, that heart of man as a race and the heart of any man as an individual is external to the Scripture.

What powerful testimony it is, then, when the Author of the Word of God gives testimony to what will happen in that cesspool of the heart when that heart comes face to face with his book, the Scriptures. When "faith cometh by hearing, and hearing by the Word of God" (Romans 10:17), and when that faith lays hold of the Word in acceptance of Christ as Saviour, that heart is changed. At the moment that the wretched heart simultaneously experiences the "sanctification of the Spirit and belief of the truth" (II Thessalonians 2:13), that heart is cleansed, made whole, indeed, changed forever! When a man in his heart, "condemned already, because he hath not believed in the name of the only begotten Son of God" (John 3:18), comes face to face with the truth of the Gospel, his heart is gloriously transformed. That one so recently a hopeless sinner becomes a saint with a lively hope. He who, moments prior was hell-bound with the potential for only evil continually, instantly becomes a "new creature: old things are passed away; behold, all things are become new" (II Corinthians 5:17).

That the Author said this would happen would give no credence to His Book, if indeed such changes never occurred. However, the alterations in the wicked hearts of multitudes who have had face-to-face and faith-to-faith encounters with the words of the Book yield external testimony to fact that the Book God wrote is filled with "words that... are spirit, and they are life" (John 6:63).

Think of the radical change in Saul who became Paul, the marvelous transformation of the Samaritan woman at Jacob's well, the one-hundred-eighty-degree turn of Crispus at the Corinthian synogogue, the miraculous work in the heart of Simon the sorcerer, and the glorious conversion of the Philippian jailor. "And what shall I more say" (Hebrews 11:32) with regard to the beautiful salvations of many at the houses of Cornelius and Lydia, on the Day of Pentecost, and in the city of Ephesus? All these and many more citations are the Author's testimony to events external to His Book which prove the power and glory of His Book.

In the twenty-first century, rife with heresy regarding the inspiration and preservation of the King James Bible, encounters with God's Book, the Bible, are still making drunkards sober, harlots lovely, druggies free, crooks honest, and Pharisees humble! Every cleansed heart in every Bible-preaching church in the world today gives external testimony to the Author that His Book is inspired and preserved.

The Answers to Waiting and Hoping. The Author's promises regarding prayer are amazing. If this entire volume were devoted to prayer and its answers, it would need to be a much larger edition. Every answered prayer, whether recorded in Scripture like Hannah's prayer for a son or never recorded for posterity to read, is a testimony by the Author about His Book, yet external to His Book. The Author said, "Ask, and it shall be given you; seek, and ye shall find; knock, and it shall be opened unto you: For every one that asketh receiveth; and he that seeketh findeth; and to him that knocketh it shall be opened" (Matthew 7:7, 8). If this promise were never obtained, the testimony of the Author would be weak. However, down through the ages, people have given testimony of millions of answers to prayers outside the scope of Scripture. This gives external testimony to the Bible that promises those answers.

Though Job waited long and grew tired, God answered his prayer. Though Saul was close and covetous, God answered David's prayer. Though the flames licked their clothing, God answered the prayers of Shadrach, Meshach and Abed-nego. Though the lions paced the cave, God answered Daniel's prayer. Though the army suffered weakness and exhaustion, God answered Hezekiah's prayer. Though all Hell seem to interfere and God seemed not to intervene, God did answer Esther's prayer. Though the government expelled them, God did answer prayers for Aquila and Priscilla. Every one of these answers and scores more were answered external to the Book. What powerful testimony!

In the twenty-first century, God still answers prayers. Every answer to prayer to understand a Scripture passage, to receive help in trials, to overcome temptation, to find comfort, to achieve goals, to meet needs, or to know God's will is an evidence outside the covers of the Book God wrote, but powerfully testifying to the truth of that Book! Each time the church meets for corporate prayer for revival and God answers with revival, there is yet another external evidence of the truth of God's Book, but external to it! Every time two or three are gathered in the name of Jesus with Him in the midst and those two or three agree on earth touching a certain thing and it is done for them by God in Heaven, there is yet another external evidence about the truth of God's Book! Every time a desperate believer, overcome by the events and circumstances of life's journey, quietly drops to his knees in the prayer closet and cries out to God in secret and the Father who sees in secret rewards him openly, there is yet one more external evidence that God's Book is inspired and preserved for this generation. No such thing as prayer and answered prayer could have come from a non-inspired, non-preserved writing of a mere man.

The Accuracy of Words and Hints. Within the scope of revelation, the Holy Ghost placed little words and hints in His prophecies that would play out in big ways in the fulfillments. With such minute details and remarkable accuracy, it is evident that God has spoken, for flawless fulfillment is beyond the realm of either coincidence or natural probability. The power of such external evidences is that men of various religious persuasions—and even some of no faith persuasion—accept that events actually developed as prophesied.

The Holy Ghost's words in Micah 5:2 include the detail of the geographical location of the birth of Christ by stating that He would be born in Bethlehem Ephratah. This signified which of the Bethlehems in Israel would be the birth site. No one with any credibility argues against the birth of the God-Man Jesus Christ in Judea's Bethlehem.

This external event lends value to the book wherein God stated the place where the event would occur seven centuries prior to its occurence.

God beautifully made known His purpose through Abraham as given in Galatians 3:16, where it is not an entire word, but a single letter that proves His revelation supernaturaly inspired and preserved: "Now to Abraham and his seed were the promises made. He saith not, and to seed were the promises made. He saith not, And to seeds, as of many; but as of one, And to thy seed, which is Christ." The perfect performance of this seemingly insignificant but truly magnificent detail is another external testimony from the Author about His Book.

Through Daniel, God gave the prophecy of specific weeks or sevens of years that would add up from the days of Daniel to the days of "Messiah the Prince" (Daniel 9:25). These weeks of years were foretold as occurring in groupings of "seven weeks, and threescore and two weeks" as outlined in Daniel's ninth chapter. External to the Book itself, these time periods accurately played out, even though Daniel spoke of this five and a half centuries before the events were completed.

Were the Scripture a normal book, such words and hints could never have occurred with such exactitude. But the Scripture is no normal book. And the Author is no normal author. The Book is the inspired, preserved record of this Author, and the Author is "the King eternal, immortal, invisible, the only wise God...the blessed and only Potentate, the King of kings, and Lord of lords; Who only hath immortality, dwelling in the light which no man can approach unto; whom no man hath seen, nor can see..." (I Timothy 1:17; 6:15, 16).

The Annals of World History. Every major or minor political or military event that was foretold in Scripture and then occurred or ever will occur is a miraculous external evidence for the validity and thus the inspiration and preservation of Scripture. The hinges of human history turn upon the doorpost of Psalm 75:6, 7 where God says, "For promotion cometh neither from the east, nor from the west, nor from the south. But God is the judge: he putteth down one, and setteth up another." Down through the ages of mankind's occupation of this earth, God has systematically and repeatedly given insights into general and specific events that would occur in the realm of the rise and fall of nations and rulers. Every such world event to which God alluded in His Word, either in sketch or in detail, has come to fruition or will do so with perfect adherence to particulars that distinguish that event so that it could be no other event. Only inspiration and preservation could accomplish that.

In Genesis 49:1, we read, "And Jacob called unto his sons, and said, Gather yourselves together, that I may tell you that which shall befall you in the last days." The remainder of that chapter gives sketchy but precise prophecy of events that were then yet future, but which are now mostly past and fulfilled. A similar passage is recorded in Deuteronomy chapter thirty-three where Moses gave his parting words to Israel. The prophet Daniel gave consummate accounts in several chapters of his book about events of the four world empires and the intertestamental period of 400 B.C. to the birth of Christ.

To the degree that the detail of these passages can be discerned, it is evident that, external to God's Word, history developed precisely as God said it would. These prophecies testify to the immutable fabric of God's Word because one can now look in retrospect and see that God "spake, and it was done" (Psalm 33:9). The student of Scripture can observe God's pre-writing of history as certain and definite; he can then consult the annals of world history and see for himself what God said through Isaiah: "Remember the former things of old: for I am God, and there is none else; I am God, and there is none like me, Declaring the end from the beginning, and from ancient times the things that are not yet done, saying, My counsel shall stand, and I will do all my pleasure....yea, I have spoken it, I will also bring it to pass; I have purposed it, I will also do it" (46:9–11).

The Internal Testimony of God About His Book. Along with speaking about things external to His Book, the Author gave extensive testimony internal to His Book. What God said in His Book about His Book is powerful testimony to its inspiration and preservation.

No Addition or Subtraction. An ancient Chinese proverb states, "Everything you add to the truth subtracts from the truth." Because God knew before the foundation of the world that His actual words would come under the Satanic attack of being added to and subtracted from, God took great pains to require that there be no addition to His

Word nor any subtraction from it. Because God knew at the outset that men would seek to add to or subtract from His inspired, preserved writings, He commanded them not to add to it or subtract from it. Because the Author understood this propensity within creation to alter perfection in a presumptuous effort to improve upon perfection, He gave internal testimony that neither addition nor subtraction from His inspired, preserved Word was permissible. Because the Author realized that any addition pollutes and any subtraction dilutes, He demanded that neither one ever take place.

Notice what the Author told Moses in the Law to tell the people: "Ye shall not add unto the word which I command you, neither shall ye diminish ought from it, that ye may keep the commandments of the Lord your God which I command you…What thing soever I command you, observe to do it: thou shalt not add thereto, nor diminish from it" (Deuteronomy 4:2; 12:32). Internal, within the Law, God gave testimony that His Work was inspired and preserved and that no man, however close to God he might be, was to add or delete "ought." Adding to or diminishing from His Book would prevent their obedience to it by changing the message. Man was, and still is, to defend the wholeness of God's Book by adamantly refusing to alter it in any fashion. Man was, and still is, to believe the Book, not investigate it, correct it, alter it, restate it, and improve it.

Give attention to what God told Solomon to tell the people in the poetical portion of the Old Testament: "Every word of God is pure: he is a shield unto them that put their trust in him. Add thou not unto his words, lest he reprove thee, and thou be found a liar" (Proverbs 30:5, 6). In this section of God's Old Testament record, He remonstrated the deletion or diminishing of even one word from His inspired, preserved record by factually stating the purity of every word. Then, from the flip side of the coin, He denounced any adding to His Words (plural) with the attached warning that doing so causes the one doing the adding to be a liar.

God told Solomon He would be a protective shield to any man who would simply trust the inspired, preserved content of His Book and would demonstrate trust in the Author by treating every single word as pure and by refraining from adding any single word. Such trust in

God excludes the trust in man that the multiversion crowd espouses. While trusting in man's scholarship may seem wise in this world, the shelter and protection of God is for those who trust him, "for vain is the help of man" (Psalm 60:11; 108:12).

Cast a glance at the prophetic announcement of God in Isaiah 29:13 and 30:1, 2: "Forasmuch as this people draw near me with their mouth, and with their lips do honour me, but have removed their heart far from me, and their fear toward me is taught by the precept of men… Woe to the rebellious children, saith the Lord, that take counsel, but not of me; and that cover with a covering, but not of my spirit, that they may add sin to sin: That walk to go down into Egypt, and have not asked at my mouth."

Isaiah spoke of a people whose religious devotion strongly resembles the attitude of religious people today: close lips and distant hearts. One reason for such hypocrisy was that those who taught that generation how to fear God were adding the precepts of men to the words of the Author of the Book. Isaiah's warning initiated by the word "woe" dealt specifically with rebellious people who were taking counsel that did not come from God's mouth. By receiving such counsel, they were adding sin to sin, that is, heaping one sin upon another. Their first sin was learning in place of God's Word the precepts of men and seeking the wrong, worldly counsel from Egypt. Because these rebellious people added the worldly counsel of Egypt to the counsel of God that Isaiah spoke to them from the mouth of God, the sin that was added onto the top of their first sin was, in a sense, adding to God's Word.

Observe Jeremiah 26:2: "Thus saith the Lord; Stand in the court of the Lord's house, and speak unto all the cities of Judah, which come to worship in the Lord's house, all the words that I command thee to speak unto them; diminish not a word." In this instance, Jeremiah was to proclaim "all the words" and "diminish not a word." Again, the Author of the inspired, preserved Word of God gave testimony from within His Book that there be no additions or subtractions.

The Lord Jesus Christ lived under the Old Testament dispensation during His earthly ministry. One of the most scathing rebukes written for us in all of the Gospels is found in Mark 7:7–9: "Howbeit in vain do they worship me, teaching for doctrines the commandments of men.

16

For laying aside the commandment of God, ye hold the tradition of men, as the washing of pots and cups: and many other such like things ye do....Full well ye reject the commandment of God, that ye may keep your own tradition." If there was ever a group that added to and subtracted from the inspired, preserved Word of God, it was the Pharisees. Their addition was that they taught for doctrines the commandments of men and kept their own traditions. Their subtraction was in that they rejected the commandment of God.

Within the scope of New Testament truth, God placed a marvelous little verse: "Brethren, I speak after the manner of men; Though it be but a man's covenant, yet if it be confirmed, no man disannulleth, or addeth thereto" (Galatians 3:15). What Paul said here is relevant to the inspiration and preservation issue facing the church in the twenty-first century. He spoke here of the legal agreements between parties or individuals in this world. The statement is that once a covenent is made, it is unalterable. Once men have written out a contract and signed it, it is legal neither to cancel it nor to take away any of its provisions nor to make additional provisions. In the case of wills, codicils may be attested, or the will may be completely renounced and a new will written, but no provision may be inserted into a legal will or detracted from a legal will once it has been signed and witnessed. If the agreement is for a sale or purchase, the same principles apply. When a homeowner agrees to sell a home in furnished condition, he cannot arbitrarily take appliances and furniture out of that home for himself. Those belong to the new buyer.

More could be said, but note that in this verse in Galatians, the power is in the fact that even among men, disannulling and adding to are prohibited. How much more is such activity prohibited when one is handling the covenant God made with man? How much more important is it that the exact covenant of God with man, authorized not with "the blood of goats and calves, but by...the blood of Christ, who through the eternal Spirit offered himself without spot to God" (Hebrews 9:12, 14) be guarded and protected? How much more egregious is it when one tampers with God's covenant by adding to it or subtracting from it after Jesus Christ has signed and notarized and sealed it with His own blood? The next paragraphs will answer just how seriously God views tamperings with His covenant.

17

The revelation to the New Testament dispensation (our dispensation) ended with perhaps the most solemn warning of all with regard to anyone's purposeful addition to and subtraction from the Scripture. The Author said, "For I testify unto every man that heareth the words of the prophecy of this book, If any man shall add unto these things, God shall add unto him the plagues that are written in this book: And if any man shall take away from the words of the book of this prophecy, God shall take away his part out of the book of life, and out of the holy city, and from the things which are written in this book."

Of all the warnings that God could have spoken in his closing breath through the last living apostle, this is what he chose. Why didn't God close the entire Scripture with a warning against sodomites and fornicators? with a warning against child predators and wifebeaters? with a warning against science falsely so called and government corruption? with a warning against covetousness and ingratitude? with a warning against lukewarmness and complacency? with a warning against Satan and the demons? Why not? Why such a strict, harsh, condemnatory word against adders and subtractors? Simple. All the other sins have their root in the sin of either adding to what God said or taking away from it or both.

Luke 24:44 outlines that Jesus Christ recognized three main divisions of the Old Testament Scripture: Law, Prophets and Psalms (poetry). There is now, of course, a fourth division of Scripture. It is the New Testament. God clearly testified in every one of these four sections that there was to be no addition and no subtraction. That is the Author's internal testimony about His Book. He took such scrupulous care to make this plain because His Word is inspired and preserved. Adding to or subtracting from His Word destroys the inspiration and prevents the preservation.

The Vernal Testimony of God About His Book. *Vernal* means "fresh or new like the spring" and thus by application, "possessing a refreshing, renewing, reviving power." The testimony of God is that His Book refreshes those who read it, and this is yet another powerful evidence that His Book is not just another book but is inspired and preserved so that men of all generations may drink its cool draught. Jeremiah said, "Thy words were found, and I did eat them; and thy word was unto me the joy and rejoicing of mine heart: for I am called by thy name, O Lord God of hosts" (Jeremiah 15:16). The miraculous nature of God's Book is that it refreshes the souls of those who read it.

George Pope Morris summed up the vernal beauty and bounty of Scripture in his poetry. He must have been one who searched its pages on a regular basis and found succour, sustenance and solace there.

> **Thou truest Friend man ever knew,**
> **Thy constancy I have tried.**
> **When all were false, I found Thee true,**
> **My Counselor and Guide.**
>
> **The mines of earth no treasure give**
> **That can this volume buy.**
> **In teaching me the way to live,**
> **It taught me how to die.**

Completed Revelation with Continual Illumination. God's miraculous Book can bring youthful revival to its readers because the abiding Holy Spirit continually shines the illuminating of His presence upon the inspired, preserved words. Were the words not both inspired and preserved, the original generation to receive them would be the only group in history to have such refreshing. However, the eager witness of thousands of years of God's people is that the Scripture continues to refresh, revive and restore. The inspiration that gave the Word of God such tremendous power remains within the pages of that Book through preservation.

Original Appropriation with Perpetual Application. In the second place, God can bring the patient reader of His Book to places of sweet revival because the Word of God has a perpetual application to life. No matter where the Christian traveler is, he can open the Scripture and find guidance. Regardless of the Christian sojourner's time in world history, he can flip through the pages of God's Book and find wisdom. What ample evidence it is that God preserved His inspired record when a saint can read today a passage he has read dozens of times and can say he has been helped every time. Was that saint enduring the same testings each time? or living under the same conditions each time? or facing the same temptations each time? or needing the same wisdom each time? or praying for the same answers each time? No. But that same passage ministered multiple and perpetual applications through its original appropriation. That could happen only through a divinely inspired, divinely preserved Book. The Author does that.

The Supernal Testimony of God About His Book. One can imagine what God is thinking about all the pompous windbags of our generation who dare to exalt themselves against the Author in their vain attempts to correct the inspired, preserved King James Bible. When God authored His Book, He placed within its text a supernal testimony; that is, a heavenly testimony from on high, as to His opinion of His Book.

Philippians 2:9–11 proclaim that "God also hath highly exalted him, and given him a name which is above every name: That at the name of Jesus every knee should bow...And that every tongue should confess that Jesus Christ is Lord, to the glory of God the Father." The pronoun *him* which occurs twice in verse nine is an obvious reference to the God-Man Jesus Christ who is cited in verses ten and eleven. The gist of this passage is that, following the seven-fold humiliation of the God-Man in the previous verses, God placed His only begotten Son in a highly exalted, heavenly position. This occurred at the ascension when Jesus Christ "was taken up, after that he through the Holy Ghost had given commandments unto the apostles whom he had chosen: To whom also he shewed himself alive after his passion by many infallible proofs...[and]...while they beheld, he was taken up; and a cloud received him out of their sight" (Acts 1:2, 3, 9). At that moment in Heaven's eternity, Jesus Christ "sat down on the right hand of the Majesty on high" (Hebrews 1:3); and there in the seat of power, he awaits the moment when "all things shall be subdued unto him" (I Corinthians 15:28).

Exalted as the Lord Jesus Christ is upon a throne above every throne, and as highly exalted as His name is above every name, yet in Heaven's understanding that has been communicated to man by the Author of the Book, there is something yet higher. The psalmist was given these inspired words, and note the treatment given to the name of God and the Word of God: "I will praise thee with my whole heart: before the gods will I sing praise unto thee. I will worship toward thy holy temple, and praise thy name for thy lovingkindness and for thy truth: for thou hast magnified thy word above all thy name" (Psalm 138:1, 2). In two short verses, the earthly writer David speaks of prais-

20

ing and worshiping the name of Jehovah God, the Lord Jesus Christ, above all the worthless, weak, wanton gods of man. In the grammatical construction, David ascribed praise to God for His loving-kindness and His truth, and then He added at the direction of the Author that the Author Himself had magnified His Word above all His name.

In essence, God has given us many names to whom honour is due. Noah, Daniel and Job are honoured in Ezekiel 14:14 and 20. Moses and Samuel are honoured in Psalm 99:6 and Jeremiah 15:1. But these names are but blips in comparison to even the least of the names of God. And of all the names of God that bring praise from the saints, the name of Jesus is at the top. And above that name, Jesus, God has magnified His Word. God testified about His Book that it is magnified; that is, made larger in appearance to the observer, than his own name! Why? The reasoning is simple. The very Word which testifies all that one can know of God must be greater than the names within it. If the Word can be discredited, then the God revealed in the Word, regardless of His name, is discredited.

The supernal testimony is plainly this: God has written a Book, the importance of which is higher than the name of Jesus Christ, the highest name in all of earth or Heaven. Truly, Jesus Christ is the living Word, and the Bible is the written Word. The King James Bible is the inspired, preserved Bible for the English-speaking world, and to tamper with its perfection is to bring inaccuracy to that which the Author has placed at the highest position of perfection and glory and preeminence.

The Eternal Testimony of God About His Book. The Author did not stop with an external testimony about what He employed men to write. Nor did He stop after giving ample internal testimony, precious vernal testimony and unequivocal supernal testimony. God had one more aspect of His testimony about His Book to include: the eternal testimony. God told us that His Book would last—and outlast.

King Solomon testified as a writer that "there are many devices in a man's heart; nevertheless the counsel of the Lord, that shall stand"; and "there is no wisdom nor understanding nor counsel against the Lord" (Proverbs 19:21; 21:30). Among the devices in the hearts of men there has always been temptation to edit and to embellish the Scriptures. In spite of all the adding and subtracting that has occurred, God's Word has stood, and English-speaking believers yet have it in its perfection in the King James Bible.

Isaiah the prophet quoted the Author of the Book who said, "My counsel shall stand, and I will do all my pleasure" (Isaiah 46:10). This amazing statement was spoken in a context of comparing the Author of the Book with all the idols of the heathen. It is a statement of the sovereignty of the Author who "declare[d] the end from the beginning, and from ancient times the things that are not yet done." Before anything ever began, God the Author knew how it would end. During the times of ancient history, God the Author knew how modern history would play out. Everything He ever said, all that He now says, and all that He ever will say are the same; and that counsel stands. That is the eternal testimony of the Author about His Book.

When Jesus Christ was here upon earth to represent His Father and to reconcile man, the creature made in the image of God, He spoke often of the Scriptures. In the much famed Sermon on the Mount, He said, "Think not that I am come to destroy the law, or the prophets: I am not come to destroy, but to fulfil. For verily I say unto you, Till heaven and earth pass, one jot or one tittle shall in no wise pass from the law, till all be fulfilled" (Matthew 5:17, 18). In His almost as famous Olivet Discourse, He said, "Heaven and earth shall pass away, but my words shall not pass away" (Matthew 24:35). As His earthly ministry drew to a close and He knew He had but hours before He would offer Himself for the sins of man, He spoke of the coming destruction of Jerusalem and the temple and of heaven and earth. To that he added that even though such destructions came and went, His Word would never be destroyed.

Beyond that, the apostles Peter and John gave corroborative revelation in II Peter 3:10–13 and Revelation 21:1 respectively of the dissolving and disappearing of the present heavens and earth; however, each of them also gave confirming testimony as to the impossibility that God's Book would dissolve or disappear. Peter said the Scripture was "a more sure word of prophecy; whereunto ye do well that ye take heed, as unto a light that shineth in a dark place" (II Peter 1:19). More sure than what? The Scripture to which Peter referred was more sure than his salvation, earthly calling and hope of Heaven (II Peter 1:10–12), more sure than his earthly life itself (II Peter 1:13–15), and more sure than the knowledge gained at the Transfiguration (II Peter 1:16, 17). The Scripture to which Peter referred was sure enough to withstand the false teachers and presumptuous brute beasts of chapter two and the scoffers and wresters of chapter three. That is due to the fact that it is inspired and preserved.

John wrote of the truth "which dwelleth in us, and shall be with us for ever" (II John 2). That truth will not pass away when believers pass away. That truth will not pass away when the heavens and earth pass away. That truth will be with us, the believers, forever. Believers will "dwell in the house of the Lord for ever" (Psalm 23:6), and they "shall...ever be with the Lord" (I Thessalonians 4:17). And that immutable truth will be with us there!

Nothing in the earthly ministry of the prophets, the Lord Jesus Christ or the apostles is any clearer than the fact that they defended the Scripture that had been given up to their time. Everything that the prophets, the Lord Jesus Christ and the apostles said in their earthly teachings points toward a higher than high regard for the Word of the Author and the Author of the Word.

Robert Grant wrote these timely and pithy lines as his testament to the high respect he had for God's Word. Today's generation could find benefit in such an attitude toward the Scriptures.

> Almighty Lord, the sun shall fail,
> The moon forget her nightly tale,
>
> And deepest silence hush on high
> The radiant chorus of the sky.
>
> But fixed for everlasting years,
> Unmoved amid the wreck of spheres,
>
> Thy Word shall shine in cloudless day
> When Heaven and earth have passed away.

In conclusion, with regard to the content of His Book, God the Author has testified externally, internally, vernally, supernally, and eternally. He has taken these great measures to communicate to us just how important His Word really is. He has emphasized to us the inspiration and preservation of His incomparable book. We twenty-first-century earth-dwellers had jolly well better think this through!

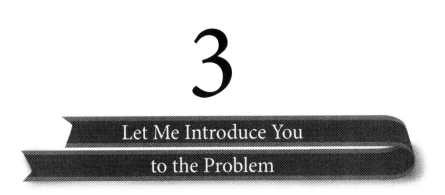

3

Let Me Introduce You
to the Problem

The controversial issues over inspiration and preservation will become non-existent when the reader of the Bible accepts the fact that the Author is God, the Lord Jehovah, the Creator of the heavens and the ends of the earth, the Holy One of Israel, the Saviour and Redeemer of man, the Head of the Church, the King of Kings and Lord of Lords, and the coming Ruler of Righteousness. When the reader of Scripture lets God be God, he has none of the problems with revelation that plague those who subconsciously lump the Author of Scripture into the pile with human authors. Neither inspiration nor preservation of Scripture pose any difficulty for the person who openly admits and acknowledges that God really is God.

Furthermore, those identical issues of inspiration and preservation pose no difficulty to the reader of the Bible who accepts the testimony of the Author about His Book. When a reader can resign himself to rest upon what God said about His own Book and resist the temptation to rely upon what man says about God's Book, he has not one question regarding inspiration and preservation.

However, if the reader does not accept that the Author of Scripture is God whose infinitudes set him apart from all other authors of all other books, the issues of inspiration and preservation become messy. Moreover, if the reader does not admit that the Author of Scripture has clearly stated that His Word would be unlike any other ever read by any man, the issues of inspiration and preservation develop into some severe spiritual headaches. And while many who wrestle in the arena of the inspiration-preservation controversy in our modern culture would not allow that they are dethroning and discrediting God, they truly are.

The root to the real problem is the type of wisdom employed in the study of Scripture origin (inspiration) and continuity (preservation). James, the austere disciple who wrote the New Testament wisdom epistle bearing his name, gave a succinct and poignant contrast in James 3:1 through 4:10 regarding the wisdom that "is from above" and the wisdom that "descendeth not from above."

The author launched into his third chapter with a stark revelation regarding the influence of teachers' tongues. From time immemorial, teachers have also been writers, using the printed page to write down for their students the content of their beliefs. Therefore, whether one uses the tongue to speak to a hearing audience or a pen to educate a reading audience makes no difference. For this reason, this chapter of *God's Forever Word* will assume a certain equality between the tongue that speaks and teaches out loud and the pen that writes down those same words for others to read and study silently.

Condemnatory Influence. First of all, James stated that the tongue and pen have the potential for condemnatory influence, that is, influence that will condemn the teacher for his wrong teaching and offend the listener who follows it! The condemnation is greater to the promoter of any false doctrine than is the offense to the receiver of that false doctrine; however, both experience damaging effects when any false doctrine is taught or written.

Inestimable damage is incurred by those who pompously raise themselves aloft in judgment of the very character of God by teaching that His Word is "not perfect," and therefore "contains errors." Those who do so from outside the faith of Jesus Christ increase their worthiness of stripes in Hell. Those who are in the faith and teach the heresy of an imperfect Bible will not be condemned with the world; but they are heaping up wood, hay and stubble works that will themselves be condemned when the Master of all good workmen calls His servants to account.

Great trouble also comes to those who receive such a sorry position as that which is taught by multiversional Bible-correctors. Because these people are taught by someone they trust, God deals less harshly with them than with the teachers. However, the condemnatory influence of wrong doctrine, in this case wrong teaching about inspiration and preservation, bears results that reach deep and far into the spiritual experience. When the lost receive the idea that the Bible is flawed and unreliable "in places," their hearts are thus hardened yet the more. One of the reasons that personal soul winners often get nowhere in their testimony is that the hearer on the other side of the door does not believe the Bible is a reliable record from God to man. When a believer receives this concept that the Bible on his coffee table, or perhaps the one in the pew rack, is a work in progress but not yet perfected, he reasons that its truths are unwarranted, its promises are unbacked, and its victory is unattainable. While the denial of the perfection of the Word of the living God will not condemn a saved soul to Hell, that denial will condemn that saved soul to an earthly life of forfeited potential and unrealized blessings.

Constructive Influence. Having established that the tongue—and thus, by definition, the pen also—of any teacher can bring condemnation and offense when used to spread false doctrine, James turned to the theme of constructive influence. A teacher of true doctrine can do much good through his tongue and pen. This teacher of true doctrine is described as "a perfect man," a term used in Scripture to classify mature believers who have grown in grace and in knowledge of God to the point that they are solidly based upon truth. The constructive influence of teachers of truth is likened to the bit in a horse's mouth and the helm of a ship. These two inventions have in common the potential to steer. The bit convinces the horse to head either right or left; the helm forces the ship to maintain or alter course. These influences are good influences, taking riders or passengers to their desired destinations, enabling the riders or passengers to avoid dangers, and so forth.

Any teacher of God's Word who bases all his teaching upon the absolute impeccability of Scripture can teach far more and far better than one who doubts Scripture veracity. The constructive influence of the faithful voice is just as inestimable for good as is the faithless voice is for evil. The constructive influence of that strong conviction does much to establish men in the faith and prepare them to stand in the evil day. The constructive influence of the faithful teacher's words, spoken or written, accomplishes much in establishing hearers and readers in the faith of our fathers.

Learners as well as teachers secure advantage in this position. The one who learns from the standpoint of a perfect Bible does not spend his time in the futile questioning of whether a passage "really says" this or that. Rather, he invests his time in the purposeful examination of the passage so that the Scripture can possess a powerful application to his own soul.

Comparative Influence. After exposing the fact that the teacher's tongue or pen can have either a good or an evil influence, James addressed the fact that the tongue—and thus the pen—has an influence that is inordinately large. The bit that steers a horse is approximately six inches long and less than a half-inch in diameter and weighs less than a pound. In comparison, a horse may be eight to ten feet in length, six or seven feet in height, eight to ten feet in girth, and may weigh well over half a ton! Monstrous ships of hundreds of feet in length are guided through waters calm or stormy by a helm that, by comparison, is generally less than one twentieth the length of the boat! So it is that the tiny tongue of the teacher is nearly insignificant by comparison to the size of its influence.

Perhaps it seems a small thing to concern oneself with whether or not he uses tongue or pen to promote the absolute perfection and preservation of the Bible, but this "very small helm" will turn about life's ship either for good or evil. No good has come from the semi-recent barrage of new translations and renditions of the Bible; instead, much evil has come about in the form of confusion and contention about what the Bible really says. Much good has come from the historical position that the Scriptures are inspired and preserved. Every sweet revival and permanent work of the Holy Spirit in the work of any believer has been accomplished by faith in an immutable revelation of God to man.

Corrupting Influence. In his ongoing treatise about teachers' tongues (and pens), James next turned to the corrupting influence. Likening the tongue to a raging, destroying fire that originated in a tiny spark barely large enough to ignite dry tinder, James demonstrated just

28

how corrupting the influence of the unchecked tongue or pen can be. Then, he moved from the idea of literal, earthly fire to the subject of literal, eternal fire. Obviously, in the context of teaching either true or false doctrine, James was proving that false doctrine has the power to corrupt both teacher and learner and send either one to the ravaging fires of Hell forever. One wonders how many sinners alive today have shelved their Bibles altogether and are no longer searching the Scriptures to find eternal life because they have heard some teacher casting shadows of doubt upon the reliability of God's Word. Furthermore, one must ask how many saints of our time are parched and scorched by the wildfires of false doctrine that have burned up their peace and left the landscape of their lives arid and barren. They are gasping their way through life without reading the Scripture for weeks at a time because they have been falsely taught that the Scripture is not reliable in its present form, nor do believers have any target date when its perfected form will be finalized.

Not only did James draw parallels between the tongue and fire, but he also showed that the tongue is like a wild animal, needing to be continually tamed. Those who "tame" wild animals, be they big cats, elephants, birds of prey, or dolphins, will readily admit that the animal is always wild. Every animal tamer is acutely aware that if he turns his back and leaves himself vulnerable, he may risk attack by an animal whose Creator gave it instincts to fear man. Just so, there must be constant vigilance over tongue and pen lest the corrupting influence of the sin nature, as ever present as an animal's instinct, take over and yield corruption. Man may turn "wild" in many ways, but attacking the perfection of the Bible will result in the most vicious mauling of men's souls imaginable.

Finally, as if to braid a threefold cord that could not be quickly broken (Ecclesiastes 4:12), James used the simile of poison to illustrate the powerful corruption inherent in one's tongue or pen. Whether strychnine from a laboratory, venom from a serpent or bacteria from spoiled food, men fear poison. No less trepidation is warranted in the presence of the tongue or pen that has inbred sinful tendencies and power. For all the wrong philosophies that men can speak and write, none bear more poison than the philosophies rooted in questions as to the veracity and immutability of Scripture.

Contradictory Influence. In the fifth place, James wrote of the contradictory influence of the tongue, that is, the strange ability that men have to talk out of both sides of their mouths. James listed four stark opposites in this portion: blessing and cursing, sweet and bitter, tree and vine, salt water and fresh. Using both plain declaration and rhetorical question, James taught that the tongue or pen can say one thing now and another later. Indeed, it seems that man is quite prone to this contradictory influence, for what man other than the God-Man, Jesus Christ, has ever lived without having uttered or written contradictory things? None!

It is in this passage that the inspiration-preservation controversy shows up in glaring brightness! Indeed, a religious—that I say not Christian—person out of one side of his mouth ascribes to God all the eternal, infinite perfections while he, out of the other side of his mouth, insists that this eternally and infinitely perfect God cannot inspire and preserve His Word to man! Such contradictory positions cannot abide, for they are as mutually exclusive as blessing and cursing are to each other.

Just as no blessing offered to God is acceptable if it is followed by a curse upon a man created by God, so there is no room for a man to praise the Almighty for His omnipotence while insisting that His omnipotence does not or cannot enable Him to preserve Scripture through time and translation. In the identical way that sweet and bitter are impossible to taste at the same time, so it is anathema to state that God is great and wonderful, but not great or wonderful enough to preserve the Scripture all the way from its prophetic, Messianic and apostolic roots until now. Even as vine fruit will never be reaped from a tree or tree fruit from a vine, so it is never going to stand up to scrutiny that God is too mighty for man to conquer but too weak to conserve His Truth. Like no fountain or spring can ever yield both salt and fresh water, so no teacher can be honest while he teaches about a God of eternal qualities whose Word is susceptible to temporal destruction.

Concealed Influence. After the shockingly revealing portion that unfolded in these verses, James finally addressed the concealed root of the entire issue, and that root is the wisdom from which that teacher teaches, whether in a classroom or in a book, whether in a sermon or in a manuscript. Opening this section with another rhetorical question, James asked who really is the wise man endued with knowledge of God? Is he the man who shows through his works the meekness of Christ, or is he the man whose bitter envying and strife is manifested in lying against the truth?

No answer is given; no answer is necessary. Everyone knows that the man who is wise and endued with the knowledge of truth as God gave it is a man whose very conversation is the meek wisdom of the Lord Himself. Everyone also knows that the man who is wise and endued with knowledge will never be one whose spirit of strife and bitterness positions himself as a liar against God's truth! The two types of wisdom are as opposite as the sweet and bitter of the previous portion. They are God's wisdom and Satan's wisdom, concealed within the soul, but clearly revealed by the tongue and pen!

There must be no shock, then, when the reader of James sees that the author said that such envying, striving, glorying, lying wisdom "descendeth not from above." Without saying so, he implied that such wisdom ascendeth up from below! The wisdom that is not from above comes bubbling up to the surface of one's soul in sulphurous stench out of the stygian darkness of Hell itself. It breaks forth upon man with blains and blisters that break out into boils. Its source is the pit of destruction.

No surprise, then, that James called this wisdom earthly, that is, worldly. The Corinthian letter lends itself to further explanation where it is written that "the world by wisdom knew not God"(I Corinthians 1:21) because God has "made foolish the wisdom of this world" (vs. 20). For all the smarts of the smartest man, he cannot know God by his smarts. For all the intellectualism of a man that will give him boldness to strive, he will find his striving against truth to be futile head-butting against Mt. Everest. For all the brilliance of a man that will embolden him to fight the truth, he will find that God makes his intelligence utterly foolish.

No marvel that James called this wisdom sensual, because of its envying, striving manner. Did not Paul castigate the Corinthians using identical words when he wrote, "For ye are yet carnal: for whereas there is among you envying, and strife, and divisions, are ye not carnal, and walk as men?" (3:3)? The word carnal used twice in the Corinthians verse is a different word than the word sensual found once in the James verse. However, by implication, they both refer to the fleshly, lower nature of man, that is, his sin nature found in his unregenerate spirit.

No wonder James wrote that this is devilish wisdom, for "from the beginning, [Satan] abode not in the truth, because there is no truth in him. When he speaketh a lie, he speaketh of his own: for he is a liar, and the father of it" (John 8:44). He lied to Eve, and he continues to lie. He can but lie. His nature is lying, his thoughts are lies, his words are lies, and his corruption of mankind proves it! The devil's wisdom on the subject of inspiration and preservation is a braggadocian, glorying wisdom that lies.

The person, however sincere, who dares to rise up and claim that the Scripture of the perfect and unassailable God contains errors, mistakes, contradictions, problems, inconsistencies, etc., is a person resting his case on wisdom that ascended up from the pit; wisdom that is earthly, sensual and devilish; wisdom first expressed in man's hearing in the words, "Yea, hath God said?" (Genesis 3:1) and, in essence, "God hath not said" (compare Genesis 3:4). Whether that person claims that the so-called errors originated at inspiration or afterward is immaterial. To describe the Bible as a mistake-riddled publication is not consistent with the nature of the God who cannot make a mistake! How fitting, then, that James declared that confusion and every evil work are found in the presence of envying and strife. No controversy touching the Christian realm in the past six thousand years has wrought more confusion and released more evil than has this concept that God's word is imperfect! The firestorm of glorying envy on the part of those who insist the Bible must be flawed is exceeded only by the firestorm of righteous indignation on the part of those who insist the Bible must be perfect!

But James was not finished. James concluded this amazing section about the tongue of the teacher—and by extension, the pen of the teacher—by taking his readers to the heights of the wisdom that is from above, the wisdom sourced and rooted in God who authored and wrote all His truth. In unparalleled Holy Ghost description, James outlined the sevenfold glory of God's wisdom. Seven is the number of perfection in all studies of biblical numerology, and its occurrence here is purposeful, not accidental!

(1) First, God's wisdom is pure. The very accusation that the Word of God is not pure from all contamination is settled here. God's wisdom, spoken from His mouth into the ears of prophet, Son and apostle alike, has been recorded in its purity. What sort of logic would allow for God to express His pure wisdom amidst the impurity of accidental omissions and inaccurate transmissions? How could God's perfection be expressed through a medium touched by that degree and type of impurity? Such inconsistency is intolerable in light of the holiness of God and illogical in light of the purity of His wisdom.

(2) Secondly, God's wisdom from above is peaceable. The word *peaceable* is an adjective meaning "salutary" or "pacific." In other words, God's wisdom produces beneficial effects and promotes curative health to the soul. God's wisdom is soothing and comforting, tending to lessen conflict in the inner man. Any person who employs faith to believe the Scriptures will find benefit and advantage to body, soul and spirit. He will be comforted. His bankruptcy will be turned to spiritual wealth; his brokenheartedness to healing; his bondage to deliverance; his blindness to sight; and his bruising to trust. The conflicts of his soul will be subdued under the solace of the inerrant Word of God. But if the Bible has mistakes, no such blessing can be sure. No such balm is found in Gilead if the aloe of Gilead is befouled by the prickers of scribal errors. No soothing coolness comes from the ointment of the apothecary if the dead flies of translators' mistakes send forth a stinking savour. Is it not obvious, dear reader, that such pleasantness from the Bible is possible only if one believes it to be flawlessly perfect?

(3) Notice in the third place that God's wisdom is gentle. The envying and strife of "worldly, sensual, devilish" wisdom is missing. In its place is the gentleness of Jesus Christ of whom it was prophesied,

> "He shall not cry, nor lift up, nor cause his voice to be heard in the street.
> " A bruised reed shall he not break, and the smoking flax shall he not quench: he shall bring forth judgment unto truth"—Isaiah 42:2, 3.

The gentleness of the wisdom of God applies in this debate about inspiration and preservation in the sense that those who accept the

Scripture as God's infallible Word possess all the closeness of the gentle shepherding of the Saviour.

(4) The next description of God's wisdom in James is the phrase *easy to be intreated*. In the direct context of James, this is doubtless a reference to the ease with which one may entreat for and receive God's wisdom: "If any of you lack wisdom, let him ask of God, that giveth to all men liberally, and upbraideth not; and it shall be given him" (1:5). The ability for any humble man or woman or boy or girl to ask God for wisdom is nowhere stated more beautifully. Those who rely completely upon the absolute perfection of Scripture do not have to wonder if a verse or passage actually communicates God's wisdom or if it is rife with errors. Rather, they can request wisdom from God; and in the sure portions of Scripture that they read, they find it.

(5) Fifth, the wisdom of God is "full of mercy and good fruits." With regard to the inspiration-preservation debate, one must see that there is no mercy extended to sinner or saint by promises in the Bible if those promises might be misworded or perhaps merely inserted by overzealous scribes. How can one obtain mercy at the throne of grace if the very words guaranteeing mercy might be mistranslated? And the good fruits? This writer has long scratched his head looking for the good fruits that have come from doubting the accuracy of the Bible. The head-scratching will continue for a long time too, because there has not been one good spiritual benefit, not one gracious outpouring of God's Spirit, not one sweet revival, not one grand conversion, and not one lovely truth from the position of doubting the purity and preservation of the King James Bible. Quite to the contrary, the inspirationist-preservationist crowd—for all the accusations of legalism and lack of love being laid upon them—are seeing, even in these days of budding apostasy and ripening world chaos, the revivals and conversions and calls of God. God honors those who honor Him, and honoring God means honoring His Word, not desecrating or discrediting it.

(6) Next to last, James wrote that the wisdom that is from God is *without partiality*. Partiality is favoritism. Simply stated, anyone can have God's wisdom. He is not partial about dispensing it. To all who ask in faith—not in intellectualistic doubting—God gives His wisdom: to plowboys or prodigies, to paupers or princes, to plebians or profes-

sors. However, the wisdom of the multiversion crowd is reserved to an elite, upper crust of studious scholars who have the lucky lot in life to possess a superior enough intellect to fathom all the supposed textual issues and "discover" God's Word through textual criticism, dynamic equivalency, "approximation translation," and, of course, a thorough working knowledge of Hebrew and Greek.

(7) Finally, in completing this sevenfold description of heavenly wisdom, James said it was without hypocrisy. Already alluded to is the "sweet water and bitter" hypocrisy of those who presume to claim that God's Word is mistaken here, unclear there and inaccurate somewhere else. No hypocrisy could be any more glaring than this. The cultural wisdom of the world, the carnal wisdom of the flesh and the cursed wisdom of the Devil all resort to hypocritical stances with regard to God's forever Word. Those who rest upon that wisdom must resort to the hypocrisy of faulting the Word of the God they claim to worship. No such hypocrisy exists in the spirit of one who pillows his soul upon the wisdom of God, believing God and every word He spoke exactly as He spoke it.

Contentious Influence. In the fourth chapter of James, yet another question is raised, but this one is not rhetorical. He answered this question about the origin of contentious wars and fightings by stating that they come out of one's warring lusts. Such contentiousness leads in one of two directions. Either the contentious individual depends upon himself to the exclusion of asking God for help, or he asks God for help for the purpose of satisfying fleshly lust. James called such people adulterers and adulteresses because of their friendship with the world, and in context he is doubtless referencing their coziness with worldly wisdom mentioned just seven verses previously!

Worldly, sensual, devilish wisdom always results in a contentious spirit. While this writer cannot categorically deny all accusations of contention within the ranks of the fundamentalism that believes in an inspired, preserved King James Bible, he can vouch for the fact that the contentious spirit on this issue is primarily on the side of the multiversion crowd that believes in a flawed Bible. The accusatory tone and acrimonious spirit of the "inaccurate Bible crowd" is as notorious as it is infamous. When it comes to inflammatory speech, they use it. When it comes to unceremonious name-calling, they call the names. When it comes to exploitive misrepresentation, they are as adept at misquoting as is the profane, liberal press.

Their contentiousness comes from the wisdom they employ, and their influence in religious and Christian circles is an influence that stirs insurrection and sparks contention! The multiversion crowds are not peacemakers because they do not rely upon peaceable wisdom. Instead, they are comprised of warring factions within the religious atmosphere of the twenty-first century. They are using both tongue and pen to release out of the same mouth both blessing and cursing, expressing via both tongue and pen the dangerous concept of an unreliable Bible that results in untamed fires, unguided ships, unbroken horses, and unsavory judgment.

Thus the problem, introduced in the first paragraphs of this chapter, is delineated. What, one might ask, is the solution? How can the contention between earthly, sensual, devilish wisdom and the wisdom that is from above be eliminated? What is the answer to tongues and pens given over to the wrong type of wisdom and thus not employing the right type of wisdom? James 4:5–10 gives a succinct and poignant fourfold wrap-up to the entire problem: (1) recognition of the spirit of man that can be drawn away by the enticement of envy; (2) reconciliation to God and His wisdom; (3) resistance against the Devil and his wisdom; and (4) restoration of fellowship whereby God and man come nigh each other. The details of this process include the cleansing of sinful hands; the purifying of double-minded hearts; and the turning of glib, flippant laughter to affliction, mourning, weeping, and heaviness. In other words, Holy Ghost revival is the real solution. Scriptural perversion through either tongue or pen of worldly wisdom will no longer be a problem when James 4:5–10 is implemented!

4

An Enemy Hath Done This

Tainted manuscripts? Who would do such a thing as to change the Word of God? to corrupt the truth? to despoil such an asset as the precious, highly valued pearl that is the Scripture? Such a question brings to mind the questions asked in the parable, "Sir, didst not thou sow good seed in thy field? from whence then hath it tares?" The answer to both queries is the same: "An enemy hath done this" (Matthew 13:27 and 28). Obviously, the parable has its direct application to the sowing of the Gospel in the world while the Devil sows his false doctrines in the world. No stretch is required, then, to apply this concept to the written record of both the pure and the tainted manuscripts under scrutiny in the inspiration-preservation debate of our day.

At issue in the inspiration-preservation arena is the written record. In the times of Bible writers, the written record was the work of scribes. The Old Testament refers to scribes fifty-four times; the New Testament, sixty-six. Generally, these one hundred twenty citations were speaking of scribes as men whose careers were devoted to copying. Their work was that of the modern-day publisher who, equipped with computer and printing press, cranks out books and pamphlets. Up to the time of the invention of the printing press, the scribes of history were people who literally made their living copying the teachings and ideas of others for the distribution of those teachings and ideas to students, disciples and other interested individuals.

Scribes made their living by writing what was dictated to them and by making handwritten copies. The content of what they copied was not of concern to them unless they were among the unique scribes like

Ezra who was "a ready scribe in the law of Moses, which the LORD God of Israel had given…a scribe of the words of the commandments of the LORD, and of his statutes to Israel…a scribe of the law of the God of heaven" (Ezra 7:6, 11, 12). Note that Ezra gave diligence to be a scribe, that is a copier, of the specific "words of the commandments of the Lord." In such fashion Ezra not only had part in the inspiration process as God gave him the Books of Chronicles and Ezra along with some Psalms, but he also had part in the preservation process as he faithfully employed himself in the accurate copying of Scripture portions so that he might "teach in Israel statutes and judgments" (Ezra 7:10) that had long been negligently overlooked and purposely avoided.

The majority of scribes did not fit the picture of loyalty to God that is found in the life of Ezra. Most of them were quite like the press of our day, latching feverishly onto any rumor or slander possible so that they might cry "Extra! Extra!" at the corners and market their wares. Such a rabid lust for news at any price is strongly indicated in Acts 23 as Paul gave his defense before Ananias and the Sanhedrin. After perceiving "that the one part were Sadducees, and the other Pharisees" (Acts 23:6), Paul claimed membership and agreement with the Pharisees. What followed was an eruption between these two warring factions of Sadducees and "the scribes that were of the Pharisees' part" (Acts 23:9). Just moments before they had been ready to skewer Paul, but they were now defending him!

Such fickle and exploitive character was characteristic of the scribes of Jesus' day. Twenty-one times in the Gospels, the scribes are mentioned alongside the Pharisees connected by the word *and*. Both were avowed enemies of Jesus Christ, seeking to trip him up in His words and no doubt writing down inaccurate records of His words to sell. Both received the same scalding rebuke from the lips of Jesus on more than one occasion. The false rumors about Christ and the apostles were given their impetus and means of propagation through the work of dishonest scribes. How else could such rumors as are recorded in Matthew 28:13 or Acts 21:28 and 38 have ever been spread?

Modern fundamentalist scholarship has invested itself in exposing both the theological heresy and the personal malfeasance of two nineteenth-century scribes, two scoundrels of manuscript corruption, namely Brooke Foss Westcott (1825-1901) and Fenton John Anthony Hort (1828-1892). These Anglican scholars at England's esteemed Cambridge University were two of the chief architects of the modern-day theory of textual criticism, and without doubt they functioned in keeping with the wisdom that "descendeth not from above" (James 3:15), as seen in the previous chapter! They were also editors of the now famous Westcott-Hort Greek Text of 1881. The Westcott-Hort Text is the text of consultation for the translations of the twentieth and twenty-first centuries.

Because of their insidious and pernicious attack against God's Word, Westcott and Hort fully deserve the castigation of fundamentalists who love the inspired, preserved Word of God. However, to limit one's understanding of who has really tainted the manuscripts to these two men is not only to give them credit they hardly deserve but also to neglect to see who has really done the dastardly deed of corrupting the Word of God.

Scripture in its miraculous origin through inspiration has always been in the crosshairs of the Devil's artillery. The enemy who has dared to sow the tares of false and corrupted manuscripts among the wheat of the faithful ones is the Devil. No one else is as bold and willing and calloused as he to pervert the Word and the words of the living God. Furthermore, let us remember that just as God's Holy Spirit fills believers to do His miraculous works, so Satan fills those who are willing vessels to do his mendacious works. And he did not wait until the second half of the nineteenth century to select Westcott and Hort to get started! Nor did he wait until 1881 to rally his minions actually to publish tainted mansucripts for the first time!

It is the contention of this writer that the vast majority of variant manuscripts are not in existence due to the oversight of a tired but otherwise faithful copyist, but due to a purposeful change. The Bible changers from time immemorial have been of at least two types: those who presumptuously attempted to improve what God said and those who viciously purposed to corrupt what God said.

The corruption or perversion of Scripture is documented in Scripture itself, and it does not require a degree in rocket science—or in higher textual criticism for that matter—to see that Satan has been in the business of questioning and perverting the truth of God for the six millennia of man's dwelling upon planet Earth. While the Old Testament with its undeveloped revelation treats the subject differently than does the New Testament, still there is a treasure trove of citations to prove that Satan has been corrupting God's message ever since God first spoke to man.

The first time that Satan entered the stage of mankind, it was for the purpose of perverting, corrupting and tainting the Word of God. No wonder Jesus said of the Devil, "He was a murderer from the beginning, and abode not in the truth, because there is no truth in him. When he speaketh a lie, he speaketh of his own: for he is a liar, and the father of it" (John 8:44). Inherent in this blistering condemnation of the enemy is the absolute principle that truth is not original with Satan, but lies are. The obverse of that is that lies are not original with God, but truth is! Just as God is the originator and the propagator of truth, so the Devil is the originator and the propagator of lies.

Tactics that were effective in the Garden of Eden are still effective, and Satan is still using them. Why should he change methods when the methods being used are so profoundly productive of the desired end? For what purpose would Satan alter his modus operandi when the manner of his deceptions is so amazingly powerful to bring about the murder he so longs to accomplish?

In the Garden of Eden, Satan questioned the inspiration and mocked the preservation of the exact message of God to Adam and Eve. He asked if God had actually said a certain thing, and then he changed what God had said to exclude and include at his will so that God's message would no longer be God's message, but his. Whether it is the Garden-of-Eden incident, the false-prophet-of-the-Old-Testament incident, the false-apostle-of-the-New-Testament incident, the Westcott-and-Hort incident, or the sodomite-translating-the-NIV incident makes no difference. The Adversary is still planting questions in the minds of people today. He is doing this by communicating to those individuals in both oral and published form that God said things He never said and did not say things that He most assuredly said. Adam and Eve were far more intelligent than any person who has ever followed them upon this planet! Their perfect knowledge had not been polluted by sin, desecrated by distance from God or befilthed by evil. Satan chose the crowning creation of God and deceived Eve by questioning inspiration and mocking preservation. He is still doing that.

In the Scripture, God backed up his mouthpieces. Who were these mouthpieces? Very simply, they were the prophets, Christ Himself and the apostles, all "holy men of God [who] spake as they were moved by the Holy Ghost" (II Peter 1:21). "God, who at sundry times and in divers manners spake in time past unto the fathers by the prophets, Hath in these last days spoken unto us by his Son" (Hebrews 1:1,2). Again, "the former treatise have I made, O Theophilus, of all that Jesus began both to do and teach, Until the day in which he was taken up, after that he through the Holy Ghost had given commandments unto the apostles whom he had chosen...speaking of the things pertaining to the kingdom of God" (Acts 1:1–3).

Still further, note that Jesus told those apostles that

> *"the Comforter, which is the Holy Ghost, whom the Father will send in my name, he shall teach you all things, and bring all things to your remembrance, whatsoever I have said unto you...But when the Comforter is come, whom I will send unto you from the Father, even the Spirit of truth, which proceedeth from the Father, he shall testify of me: And ye also shall bear witness, because ye have been with me from the beginning...I have yet many things to say unto you, but ye cannot bear them now. Howbeit when he, the Spirit of truth, is come, he will guide you into all truth: for he shall not speak of himself; but whatsoever he shall hear, that shall he speak: and he will shew you things to come. He shall glorify me: for he shall receive of mine, and shall shew it unto you. All things that the Father hath are mine: therefore said I, that he shall take of mine, and shall shew it unto you...For I have given unto them the words which thou gavest me; and they have received them...I have given them thy word"* (John 14:26; 15:26, 27; 16:12–15; 17:8,14).

Ephesians 2:20 is a New Testament revelation that sums up the whole issue. The church is "built upon the foundation of the apostles and prophets, Jesus Christ himself being the chief corner stone." Therefore, to question Moses or Jeremiah was to question God, because these men had God's Word coming from their mouths. To undermine the Lord Jesus Christ was to undermine the Father in Heaven, because Jesus not only spoke God's Word, but He was and is God's Word. To challenge the apostles was to challenge God himself, because the apostles were God's chosen spokesmen to record fulfilled prophecies of the Old Testament, to testify of Christ in his actual humanity and in his resurrected reality, to command the church of true believers for the age of grace, and to prophesy of that which is still future even as we speak and write.

The Prophets. Seventy-four times in the Pentateuch alone a reader may find the words "the Lord spake unto Moses, saying…" Dozens more times, some variation of those words is found. Unquestionably, God spoke through Moses. Later in the prophets, God's Word says, "Samuel grew, and the Lord was with him, and did let none of his words fall to the ground. And all Israel from Dan even to Beer-sheba knew that Samuel was established to be a prophet of the Lord. And the Lord appeared again in Shiloh: for the Lord revealed himself to Samuel in Shiloh by the word of the Lord" (I Samuel 3:19–21). None but infidels would deny that God spoke through Samuel.

And who would doubt that God spoke through David the precious words of many of the Psalms? Not God. It was God who plainly said of His chosen king and the man after His own heart, "Now these be the last words of David. David the son of Jesse said, and the man who was raised up on high, the anointed of the God of Jacob, and the sweet psalmist of Israel, said, The Spirit of the Lord spake by me, and his word was in my tongue. The God of Israel said, the Rock of Israel spake to me" (II Samuel 23:1–3).

Regarding the prophets whose ministries are recorded in books of Scripture bearing their names, there can be no doubt that they were God's mouthpieces. Consider that God recorded such proofs as the following: "At the same time spake the Lord by Isaiah the son of Amoz" (Isaiah 20:2); "And the Lord said unto me, Behold, I have put my words in thy mouth" (Jeremiah 1:9); "The word of the Lord came expressly unto Ezekiel the priest" (Ezekiel 1:3); "The word of the Lord that came unto Hosea…The beginning of the word of the Lord by Hosea" (Hosea 1:1, 2); and so on. The Book of Jeremiah has in excess of forty references stating either "the word of the Lord came unto me," or "the word that came unto me from the Lord," or some variation thereof. Ezekiel's prophecy contains over one hundred twenty instances of the words, "Thus saith the Lord God," an authoritative qualifier ascribed another forty times to messages from God given to Moses, Joshua, Samuel,

Nathan, Elijah, Elisha, Isaiah, Jeremiah, and Amos. Two hundred fifty more times, Scripture records the words, "Thus saith the Lord." Only the Devil and his vicious cohorts among the infidels and pagans and rebels of the ages would refuse to admit that God spoke to and by his prophets. An enemy hath done this.

The Son of God, Jesus Christ. God spoke to us by Jesus Christ also. He who was and is and ever shall be the living Word gave us the spoken and written Word. For the Son of God and Son of Man to have been called the Word is manifest evidence of His Father's speaking through Him. To the apostle John was given exclusive right to name Christ the Word. In three of the five books of Scripture ascribed to him, John refers to the Lord Jesus as the Word with the capitalized *w*.

In His earthly ministry, Jesus Christ said such things as are indisputable evidence of the Father's Word in the Son's mouth. Hebrews 10:5–9 record a preincarnation conversation between the Father and the Son in which the Lord Jesus Christ confirms the Word of God penned by David the psalmist prophet. From that moment to the very first recorded words of His earthly sojourn—"How is it that ye sought me? wist ye not that I must be about my Father's business?" (Luke 2:49)—until his seven utterances upon the cross and His final commission to the disciples prior to his ascension, Scripture proves that the Lord Jesus Christ upon earth spoke for His Father in Heaven. Consider that he said, "My doctrine is not mine, but his that sent me" (John 7:16); "I have many things to say and to judge of you: but he that sent me is true; and I speak to the world those things which I have heard of him" (John 8:26); "For I have not spoken of myself; but the Father which sent me, he gave me a commandment, what I should say, and what I should speak. And I know that his commandment is life everlasting: whatsoever I speak therefore, even as the Father said unto me, so I speak" (John 12:49,50); and "...the word which ye hear is not mine, but the Father's which sent me" (John 14:24). Either the Lord Jesus Christ was a consummate liar, or he spoke the exact words that God the Father administered for Him to say upon earth—adding nothing, detracting nothing, changing nothing! This author stands solidly with the latter. Any denial of the God of Heaven speaking through His only begotten Son, is another proof that an enemy hath done this.

This poor sinner who has, by the grace and mercy of God, become a consecrated saint and a called servant of Jesus Christ rests his salvation and all his life and all his eternity upon the words of this same Jesus who said, "Verily, verily, I say unto you, He that heareth my word, and believeth on him that sent me, hath everlasting life, and shall not come into condemnation; but is passed from death unto life" (John 5:24). If these are not the Father's words, whose are they? Are these words some myth, some fable, some deceptive contrivance to lull unsuspecting souls into a lifetime of lethargy, only to snatch them from the gates of Heaven at the end and shove them through the gates of Hell? To paraphrase a popular news maxim of our day: This writer reports. You decide.

The Apostles. Apostolic revelation is full of the authority of God. Beginning with the Book of Matthew and continuing through the Book of Revelation, God has given us twenty-seven apostolic writings. Replete in these Gospels, Epistles and prophecies are the words "that it might be fulfilled which was spoken by the prophet" and "it is written" and so forth. These citations of Old Testament passages demonstrate that the New Testament is not a contradiction of or an improvement upon, but a fulfillment of some things and a fuller revelation of others found in Scripture.

Did not the Lord Himself tell His apostles that "many prophets and kings have desired to see those things which ye see, and have not seen them; and to hear those things which ye hear, and have not heard them" (Luke 10:24)? The apostle Peter, in direct agreement with his Saviour and Lord, wrote of undisclosed mysteries of the Old Testament that were made fully clear in the New Testament when he mentioned the salvation which "the prophets have inquired and searched diligently, who prophesied of the grace that should come unto you: Searching what, or what manner of time the Spirit of Christ which was in them did signify, when it testified beforehand the sufferings of Christ, and the glory that should follow" (I Peter 1:10, 11). On top of telling us that the Spirit of Christ spoke through the Old Testament prophets, Peter attested to the completion of revelation through the apostles.

Having established that God most certainly has spoken, and that He has spoken through the prophets, through Christ His only begotten

Son and through the apostles, the narrative of this chapter can now return to the subject raised by the title and its early paragraphs. An enemy has crept in and changed what God has said, and that enemy is surely Satan, the Devil, the adversary, the tempter, the wicked one, the liar and father of all lies! As surely as God has spoken through prophets and His Son and the apostles, Satan has spoken through his mouthpieces down through the centuries of created time to twistedly thwart and perniciously pervert that very Word from God's mouth. As surely as God has written down what He said and preserved it, Satan has written down close but perverted facsimiles of what God said. "Now as Jannes and Jambres withstood Moses, so do these also resist the truth: men of corrupt minds, reprobate concerning the faith" (II Timothy 3:8). An enemy hath done this.

Corrupted Gospels. Consider a little gem, the word *many,* in Luke 1:1. According to tradition and respected chronologies, the dates of writing for the four Gospel accounts are as follows: Matthew in A.D. 37, Mark in A.D. 57–63, Luke in A.D. 63–68 and John in A.D. 85–90. With these accepted dates in mind, it is evident that two of the gospel records were penned prior to Luke's and one afterward. With regard, then, to the opening statement of the beloved physician in Luke 1:1–4, he told us, "Forasmuch as many have taken in hand to set forth in order a declaration of those things which are most surely believed among us, Even as they delivered them unto us, which from the beginning were eyewitnesses, and ministers of the word; It seemed good to me also, having had perfect understanding of all things from the very first, to write unto thee in order, most excellent Theophilus, That thou mightest know the certainty of those things, wherein thou hast been instructed."

Luke says that, at his writing, many other writers had already begun to write out a personal history of Christ, a gospel if you please (e.g. the recently published, highly marketed and much exalted gospel according to Judas Iscariot), of the events believed among the first-century Greeks and Romans, some of whom were believers. While the dates of writing of the four canonical Gospels cannot be absolutely fixed, even if all three other Gospels were written before Luke's, three is not many. Certainly two Gospels written before his cannot be deemed as many. Evident in Luke's Spirit-inspired use of the word many is that there were many writers attempting to set down in published form a biography of

45

Jesus Christ, the Son of Man and Son of God.

One might question just what could be wrong with such an effort. What could be the problem with someone's jotting down for future generations his own personal memories and recountings of the words and works of the Lord Jesus Christ? Would not such multiple characterizations and portrayals of our blessed Lord be enlightening, presenting him from several different angles and viewpoints? Could not the student of Scripture, yea, the disciple of Jesus Christ, know more of Him were he to have twenty Gospels at his disposal instead of the measly four? That would be the opinion of intellectualist scholars who have lived in every generation, but it was evidently not the opinion of the Author of Scripture. God the Holy Ghost decided that there would be four human writers whom he would endue with supernatural power so that all the facts were accurate and perfect.

What that means is that of the *many* whom Luke references in Luke 1:1, only two to that date (Matthew and Mark), himself and one after him (John) were Holy-Ghost-inspired writers. All the others were merely men relying upon their own perspectives to opine, their own abilities to recall, their own slanted opinions to evaluate, etc. That means that whether those others of Luke's *many* (aside from Matthew, Mark, John, and himself) intended to corrupt the truth or whether they were innocently recording what they remembered, their accounts were not wholly truthful. Those others of the many were open to the influence of Satan, the corrupter of manuscripts, the enemy who hath done this. Those others were exposed to the influence of the flesh, their own darkened hearts defiled by sin. Those others were vulnerable to the influence of the world and all its philosophical poison and deception. Those others were subject to the infirmities of flawed memory, gilded experience, limited understanding, and unreliable deduction.

While those other men may have had good intention to pen the events and words surrounding the Lord Jesus Christ, their efforts were not hemmed in by the Holy Spirit who Jesus said would "bring all things to your remembrance, whatsoever I have said unto you" (John 14:26); who Jesus said would "guide you into all truth: for he shall not speak of himself" (16:13); so that the result would be that "the word which ye hear is not mine, but the Father's which sent me" (14:24).

That is just the point. The word which we read in the four Gospels is not the words of Matthew, Mark, Luke and/or John. The word we read there is the Word of God: Father, Son and Holy Spirit, who are the Author of Scripture. That promised Holy Spirit brought everything perfectly to the remembrance of those four and no more. He guided their writing into all truth, but He did not do that for the "many" others. Luke pointed out in the four opening verses of his Gospel that the things which he wrote had been delivered to him. Who delivered them to him? The Holy Ghost of God, the third person of the Godhead, delivered to Luke those truths most surely believed among the first-century Christians. Luke said that he possessed perfect understanding of all the things from the very first. Where did he get such perfect understanding of every detail he wrote? Though he was a well-educated and respected physician, he did not possess "perfect understanding from the very first" through scholarly study, through impressive intellectual capacity, or even via a photographic memory. He got that perfect understanding from the Holy Spirit. For that reason and that reason alone, he could authoritatively say that Theophilus could "know the certainty of those things" wherein he had been instructed. Incidentally, that is the only way any of us know the certainty of those things of the Scripture wherein we have been instructed. The Holy Spirit authored those things in inspiration, and ever since, godly men have written and copied and translated them under preservation, and praise God we have today an accurate record of "those things which are most surely believed among us," and we can know the certainty of those things.

As to the *many* of Luke 1:1, let it be understood that there are many flawed and inaccurate accounts regarding the Lord Jesus Christ's birth, His earthly sojourn, His ministry and miracles, and His teachings and doctrine. However, the greatest disparity is found in the many imperfect writings of His sacrificial death and blood atonement and of His resurrection and ascension. Satan, the corrupter of all truth and father of all lies, wishes most to disparage Christ's paying for our sins and His rising from the dead. Satan little cares if a man believes that Jesus walked in Galilee, healed the sick and taught beatitudes to the multitudes. He much cares if that same man believes that Jesus died for his sins and rose for his justification.

The many false gospels have abounded for centuries. Their corrupted content is indicated in passages such as Matthew 27:62–66 and

28:11–15. Some are Greek or Egyptian, full of worldly ideology and inaccurate lines of reasoning. Some are Jewish or Catholic, replete with religious slant and agenda-laden twists. Some are liberal with the intent of discrediting faith; others are political with the goal of inciting social activism and public rebellion. Some are even immoral, allowing that Christ might have been an adulterer with Mary Magdalene and other women, a sodomite with John, or even a pedophile due to His frequent contact with children. Most, if not all, of them contain some truth; however, none of them contain truth exclusively except for Matthew, Mark, Luke, and John. An enemy hath done this.

Corrupted Epistles. In addition to corruptions in the gospel accounts that were written concurrent with the true Gospels, there was contemporary corruption of the epistles to the churches and pastors. The examples of this are many; the following citations will serve to prove that Satan has certainly been corrupting manuscripts for thousands of years.

To the Church at Thessalonica. Paul addressed the Thessalonian church with an enlightening concept in his second epistle. Clear evidence and reliable dating combine to place both of the Thessalonian letters in A.D.54, so the two missives were written a maximum of twelve months apart from one another. In II Thessalonians 2:2, Paul implores the new believers in that young church to "be not soon shaken in mind, or be troubled, neither by spirit, nor by word, nor by letter as from us, as that the day of Christ is at hand." This verse reveals to the enlightened reader that by three insidious and divisive methods, the Devil who questions all inspired, preserved Scripture had crept into the Thessalonian church. By means of spirits (note that the s is not capitalized, nor does the definite article the precede the word spirit to identify this as the Holy Spirit), words, and letters, the Thessalonian believers had been shaken in mind and troubled. An enemy hath done this.

Within the short space of twelve months or less, Satan had spiritually bombarded these new believers with troubling, soul-shaking doubts about the coming of Christ. This he had accomplished by dispatching demons, unclean spirits, foul spirits, spirits of divination, lying spirits, and a host of other corrupted, evil spirit beings to have access to the thinking processes of the members of that church. Beyond that, he had sent wolves in sheep's clothing to their assembly to speak words of confusion and fear to the believers. And furthermore, he had used some to write letters "as from us," that is, letters that so closely resembled the inspired, preserved letters from Paul that the new believers at Thessalonica thought they were from Paul, and so they believed them. What is this if it is not corrupting of manuscripts? No wonder Paul closed his second communique to them with "the salutation of Paul with mine own hand, which is the token in every epistle: so I write" (II Thessalonians 3:17). He did this so that from that day on the believers there would be able to identify the true from the false and realize that an enemy hath done this.

To the Churches of Galatia. A few years later, Paul wrote to the churches of Galatia. This province was located in what is the eastern half of modern-day Turkey. Peter ministered there in person as I Peter 1:1 clearly indicates. In Paul's writings to the churches of that province, he addressed the issue of false doctrine: "I marvel that ye are so soon removed from him that called you into the grace of Christ unto another gospel: which is not another; but there be some that trouble you, and would pervert the gospel of Christ. But though we, or an angel from heaven, preach any other gospel unto you than that which we have preached unto you, let him be accursed. As we said before, so say I now again, If any man preach any other gospel unto you than that ye have received, let him be accursed" (Galatians 1:6–9). In so many words, Paul was admitting that an enemy hath done this.

What was this perverted gospel that the Galatians were receiving? What were its contents? Obvious from the text of Galatians 2:1–5, the perverted gospel was the Judaizers' gospel, a gospel that included circumcision as a requirement for salvation. The spokespersons for that impure gospel were "false brethren unawares brought in" (Galatians 2:4) who addressed the congregations as they had opportunity. Furthermore, this false gospel was a gospel that required separation from uncircumcised people in public eating situations. So strong was the pull of this false gospel that even Peter and Barnabas (Galatians 2:11–13) were temporarily ensnared by it. It was Paul who noted that even "they walked not uprightly according to the truth of the gospel" (Galatians 2:14). Where did such ideas originate? Again, the spokesmen were those who "bewitched [them], that [they] should not obey the truth"

(Galatians 3:1). These false doctrinal concepts came from the Devil who, even as early as A.D. 58 (the accepted date of Paul's writing to the Galatians) had corrupted the inspired, preserved message of the Gospel. An enemy hath done this.

That these Judaizing, circumcision-preaching, law-keeping, false gospelizers were writing to the Galatian believers and corrupting the manuscripts received from the apostles Peter and Paul is evident from the beginning of the Galatian Epistle where Paul felt compelled to say, "Now the things which I write unto you, behold, before God, I lie not" (Galatians 1:20). Note next that he said in Galatians 3:15, "Brethren, I speak after the manner of men; Though it be but a man's covenant, yet if it be confirmed, no man disannulleth, or addeth thereto." Confirmed covenants that could not be altered by disannullment or addition were written covenants. Furthermore, Paul takes pains at the end of this letter to emphasize, "Ye see how large a letter I have written unto you with mine own hand" (6:11) in an effort to distinguish between the one true manuscript from the true apostle and the many false manuscripts from false apostles. Obvious to discerning readers is that some were taking the writings of the apostles of Christ and cleverly rewording them with small and hard-to-discern additions and deletions in their effort to teach a false gospel and a false Christian ethic. What is this if it is not corrupting of manuscripts? An enemy hath done this.

To the Church at Corinth. On another occasion, Paul the apostle addressed the Corinthian church, a carnal group whose eighteen months under Paul's tutelage and discipleship resulted in less spiritual growth than the Thessalonians exhibited in three weeks! The two letters to this church are traditionally dated A.D. 59 and 60. This means the gap between them could have been as little as a month or two or as much as twenty-four months. At any rate, Paul speaks of naive, gullible willingness on the part of the Corinthians to "suffer fools gladly" (II Corinthians 11:19) to be their preachers and pastors. These fools, Paul had just told them, were "false apostles, deceitful workers, transforming themselves into the apostles of Christ. And no marvel; for Satan himself is transformed into an angel of light. Therefore it is no great thing if his ministers also be transformed as the ministers of righteousness" (vss. 13–15). It is no surprise then that just previous to that, Paul had expressed his deep concern that "as the serpent beguiled Eve through his subtilty, so [their] minds should be corrupted from the simplicity that is in Christ" (vs. 3).

How did the serpent beguile Eve through his subtlety? In Genesis, chapter three, he questioned the inspiration of Scripture when he asked, "Yea, hath God said, Ye shall not eat of every tree of the garden?" In that same chapter, he caused Eve to question the preservation of Scripture when he added to and took away from the exact words of what God had said. Eve's confusion about what God had said did not come from God but from Satan. His adding all the trees to the prohibition of eating from the tree of knowledge of good and evil confused Eve. Even though she corrected Satan's misrepresentation and told him that the prohibition was for only one tree, she was muddled to the degree that she added a prohibition of touching the tree.

Then Satan took away from God's revelation when he told Eve, "Ye shall not surely die." He then added to God's clear word again when he said, "For God doth know that in the day ye eat thereof, then your eyes shall be opened, and ye shall be as gods, knowing good and evil." This information God had never spoken to Adam and Eve. Satan was lying to Eve through the means of casting doubt upon the inspiration of God's very words and by means of adding just enough and taking away just enough to make what God had said say something else.

This was the concern of the apostle Paul for the Corinthians. He was deeply moved within for the souls from Corinth whom he had brought to Christ, whom he loved, and in whom he longed to see spiritual growth. He feared that fools who occupied the Corinthian pulpit were false apostles, communicating to his beloved converts a false message in their words and letters. He agonized over the fact that the "fools" whom the Corinthians permitted to be their instructors were deceitful workers pretending to be Christ's apostles and ministers of righteousness when they were actually Satan's mouthpieces to dislodge the pure message and word of I Corinthians from the church. Paul was indeed persuaded that "an enemy hath done this."

Vulnerable Pastors. Not only were the specific epistles to actual local church bodies of the first century corrupted by enemy-promoted manuscripts, but the first-century pastors themselves were also the targets of corruption through perverted teachings and writings.

51

Timothy and Titus. When Paul wrote to Timothy, he commanded his young preacher son to "charge some that they teach no other doctrine, Neither give heed to fables and endless genealogies, which minister questions, rather than godly edifying which is in faith" (I Timothy 1:3,4). This would have been an irrelevant command if no other doctrines were being copied and circulated, if no disciples of Christ were listening to fable doctrines, if no enemy preachers and writers were causing questions among the believers about the truth, or if all the believers were already being edified in the true faith.

Furthermore, he cautioned Timothy that some would "depart from the faith, giving heed to seducing spirits, and doctrines of devils; Speaking lies in hypocrisy; having their conscience seared with a hot iron" (4:1, 2). This would have been a moot caution to Timothy if none would depart from the faith due to perverted teachings and writings, if none would listen to false doctrines spawned in the minds of false teachers and writers by seducing spirits, if none of the false preachers and writers spoke lies.

In his letter to Titus, he referred to "many unruly and vain talkers and deceivers, specially they of the circumcision: Whose mouths must be stopped, who subvert whole houses, teaching things which they ought not, for filthy lucre's sake...Wherefore rebuke them sharply, that they may be sound in the faith; Not giving heed to Jewish fables, and commandments of men, that turn from the truth" (Titus 1:10–14). Such words to Titus would have been unnecessary fear mongering were there no such individuals in Crete spreading the deceptive messages. Those teaching for filthy lucre's sake were undoubtedly writers who sold their printed messages. They were like the false teachers whom Peter cited, who "through covetousness...with feigned words make merchandise" (II Peter 2:3) of unsuspecting hearers and readers.

While much of the content of the Pastoral Epistles to Timothy and Titus addresses the subject of oral preaching and teaching, it is unthinkable that those who departed from the true revelation of God due to their seared consciences and who publicly spoke hypocritical lies did not also write out their beliefs and circulate them. Who ever heard of fables or genealogies or commandments that were limited to speech and not written down and spread around? What society relies completely upon verbal tradition and does not write down its beliefs? How was filthy lucre associated with teaching if it was not in the selling of scrolls and parchments that contained the teachings of the heretics? Certainly the Greek and Roman cultures were some of the most prolific in the writing of their philosophies, and it is ludicrous to suppose that the ideas of those corrupters were never written. What is this if it is not corrupting of manuscripts? An enemy hath done this.

The apostle Paul even named some of those who were most pernicious in the circulating of their perverted teachings. In this cataloguing of these particular men, he warned Timothy—and ensuing generations including ours—of four types of corruption in manuscript evidence.

Hymenaeus and Alexander—Blasphemous Corruption. The first example is the blasphemous corruption of the true record of God's Word. The apostle Paul listed Hymenaeus and Alexander in I Timothy 1:20 as men who had "put away" a good conscience "concerning faith" and had "made shipwreck"; small wonder then that the Spirit-filled apostle delivered them both "unto Satan, that they may learn not to blaspheme." If the Bible student allows Scripture to govern Scripture (as he well should), he will note that deliverance to Satan was both an apostolic matter as well as a church matter (I Corinthians 5:3–5). In the case of the immoral man in the Corinthian church, the deliverance to Satan was for the moral purity of the church body. The situation with Hymenaeus and Alexander, however, was a deliverance unto Satan for the spiritual purity of the truth contained in inspired, preserved manuscripts which the two false teachers had so diligently corrupted in their efforts to dissuade their followers of God's truth and persuade them of Satan's lies. An enemy hath done this.

Hymenaeus and Philetus—Erroneous Corruption. Paul next mentioned the blasphemer Hymenaeus in II Timothy 2:17 along with another infamous, first-century apostate named Philetus in an example of erroneous corruption of the truth of God. In this reference, the two are accused of circulating "profane and vain babblings," the content of which ate up the immature believers "as doth a canker," with the ultimate result being that these young Christians would "increase unto more ungodliness." Hymenaeus and Philetus did this by teaching and promoting the error that "the resurrection is past already." While such an absurdity might smack of the ridiculous to a seasoned believer, a young, immature believer might easily be led astray and overthrown by such clever contrivances. A bit of adding to one passage and a bit of subtracting from another could easily accomplish the appearance that the resurrection is a past event, not a future one.

Of course, much sin arises out of false teachings and writings about the resurrection, as is clear from I Corinthians 15:33,34: "Be not deceived: evil communications corrupt good manners. Awake to righteousness, and sin not; for some have not the knowledge of God: I speak this to your shame." Evil communications, whether spoken or written, corrupt the good behavior of God's people in any generation. When one is lulled to sleep with regard to inspired, preserved resurrection truth, he turns to sinful living and lethargy with regard to urgent evangelism. Not only are both of these shameful pursuits for either the believer or the church, but they are also both the goal and hope of manuscript corrupters! An enemy hath done this.

Alexander—Disputatious Corruption. When Paul next cited Alexander, it was in II Timothy 4:14,15: "Alexander the coppersmith did me much evil: the Lord reward him according to his works: Of whom be thou ware also; for he hath greatly withstood our words." Paul was not warning Timothy about a man who had an isolated argument with Paul about some remote text of Scripture. He was warning his young preacher son about a man whose work was the teaching, promoting and publishing of error in direct opposition to God's words of truth from the mouth and pen of Paul.

If Alexander had been limited to actual audiences of his oral teaching, his potential to do Paul much evil would have been real. However, with the employment of scribes to write out and publish his works and circulate them, he certainly had far more power to do Paul evil. Furthermore, as Paul was aging and soon to die, so Alexander would one day die. But the perverted manuscripts and tainted writings of Alexander would live on and continue to be copied and distributed long into the ministry years of the younger Timothy. An enemy hath done this.

Phygellus and Hermogenes—Malicious Corruption. These two men's single reference in Scripture reads, "This thou knowest, that all they which are in Asia be turned away from me; of whom are Phygellus and

Hermogenes" (II Timothy 1:15). Phygellus and Hermogenes may very well have been the leaders in this doctrinal insurrection. Let's assume that's the reason they are named and called out here.

While being "of Paul...of Apollos...of Cephas...and...of Christ" was rebuked as contentious divisiveness and carnal envy in I Corinthians 1:10–13 and 3:1–4, being "of Paul" in any sense of promoting and defending the inspired, preserved faith was the right position because Paul was God's apostolic mouthpiece for revelation of church-age truth. Indeed, these same believers in Corinth were told to be "of Paul" in the right context when Paul later wrote, "Be ye followers of me, even as I also am of Christ" (I Corinthians 11:1). This latter text proves that when one is doctrinally and practically right, being "of Paul" is also being "of Christ."

For Phygellus and Hermogenes to turn away all those who were in Asia from Paul's position was cruel at best, paralleling the sedition of Absalom who "stole the hearts of the men of Israel" (II Samuel 15:6). Phygellus and Hermogenes stole the hearts of the disciples of Asia from Paul. It had been through Paul's two-year ministry of daily and diligently preaching and teaching at the school of Tyrannus in the synogogue at Ephesus "that all they which dwelt in Asia heard the word of the Lord Jesus, both Jews and Greeks" (Acts 19:10). That this was a malicious corruption is clear from the words "turned away from me" in the reference. Phygellus and Hermogenes' efforts to corrupt the spoken teachings and the written manuscripts of Paul the apostle were accomplished by their turning the people away from Paul personally. This they did by some means of personal slander that caused "all they... in Asia" gradually to grow from respecting Paul to detesting him and turning away from him to follow the two imposters.

Their influence in Asia was no doubt the seed that germinated, grew and bore fruit so that some thirty years later, John had to write rebukes to six of the seven churches of Asia. And what were John's rebukes about? Were those rebukes about personalities? No. John spoke deliberately and decisively to those churches about their doctrine, citing the churches at Ephesus and Pergamos for Nicolaitanism, the church at Smyrna for blasphemy, the churches at Pergamos and Thyatira for idolatry and fornication, the church at Sardis for deadness, and the church at Laodicea for apathy and apostasy. What reason can be any more fundamental to the growth of these false doctrines than the corrupting of the inspired, preserved Word of God? An enemy hath done this.

Pastors in Pontus, Galatia, Cappadocia, Asia, and Bithynia. In about A.D. 66, Peter wrote to the pastors among the dispersed believers of the region now known as Turkey. His second epistle is at once a declaration on the defensive for the truth of God and a declaration on the offensive against false teachers. In the first three verses of the second chapter, preserved for the saints of every generation, he makes a scathing rebuke of false teachers who "privily…bring in damnable heresies, even denying the Lord that bought them." Peter continued to accuse these liars as ones who would through "feigned words make merchandise" of believers. Peter's lament through Holy Ghost inspiration was that "many shall follow their pernicious ways."

Again, it would be ludicrous to suppose that these sneaky false teachers would not have used the medium of publication. Doubtless, they procured copies of the true words of the apostles and doctored those manuscripts in clever, subtle manner. Then, they republished the manuscripts and distributed them to the same believers whom Peter had attempted to disciple. That we do not have a clear declaration of this process is no proof that manuscript corruption did not occur; that Peter warns his readers (and thus believers today) that "there shall be false teachers among you, who privily shall bring in damnable heresies" is proof that manuscript corruption did occur.

The degree of manuscript corruption to which Peter referred was enough to teach the denial of the deity of Christ (vs. 2). This is indeed a damnable heresy (vs. 1), that is, a heresy that has potential to damn souls to Hell. Indeed if Christ be not God, there is no salvation! The manuscript corruption against which Peter warned was also to the extent that the false teachers among them were likened to the angels that sinned, to the wicked of Noah's day, to the sodomites, and to the despisers of human authority down through the ages (vss. 4–11). The reach of this manuscript corruption affected the hearers and readers even to the point of compromising Christian morality, honest integrity and biblical liberty (vss. 12–22). No honest conclusion can miss the fact that Peter is saying, "An enemy hath done this."

Jude also wrote in A.D. 66 of the pressing need to write to the saints that they "should earnestly contend for the faith which was once delivered unto the saints" (vs. 3). The reason he gives for such an urgent exhortation to all believers is that there were "certain men crept in unawares, who were before of old ordained to this condemnation, ungodly men, turning the grace of our God into lasciviousness, and denying the only Lord God, and our Lord Jesus Christ" (vs. 4).

While it may be true that Christians use clandestine means to get Bibles into closed countries, that is not the context of Paul's or Jude's rebukes. Paul and Jude were clearly citing the deceptiveness of false preachers and teachers. In such a context, one might ask, What prophet of God or apostle of Jesus Christ had to be sneaked in to give his message? When has God ever used delusion, deceit, creeping around, and sliding under doors undetected to get His Gospel and His truth to His people? NEVER! An enemy hath done this. And the enemy is Satan.

In conclusion, it is clearly evident that, despite all the hermeneutical hat tricks and lexicographical legerdemain of the textual critics, God has both inspired and preserved His Word. It is just as clearly evident that Satan has been corrupting God's Word for millennia. He is the true enemy who hath done this, and the corrupted manuscripts that have mysteriously come out of the woodwork to serve as the backdrop for every new translation of the past century are but the recurrences and rediscoveries of his corruptions begun so long ago.

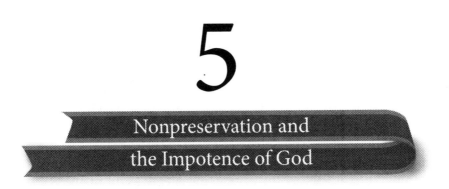

5

Nonpreservation and the Impotence of God

Nonpreservationist theory in regard to God's maintenance of a perfect Scripture demands an impotent God. Multiversionism as it pertains to God's oversight of an unchanged and unchanging Bible requires a weak, powerless God. The absolute omnipotence of God has been addressed already in Chapter One with regard to the Author of Scripture. The focus of this chapter is the evidence of the omnipotence of God in His preservation ability in several areas as well as the evidence that an inability to preserve the Scripture would demand impotence on His part.

Preservation requires sovereign power. God possesses sovereign power. Intellectualists and humanists deny sovereign power. Intellectualists and humanists denigrate sovereign power. To them, because sovereign power is not visible under a microscope, explainable in a laboratory experiment, or definable in a scholastic theorem, it is unreasonable and unreliable. Intellectualists and humanists have allowed their superior air to convince them of their ability—indeed their calling—to investigate what they claim are the errors of Scripture and then decide what God really said. They pretend to do this by processes that are worthy in the study of the amoeba, but not in the study of the autographa!

Scripture is a miracle! It is a miracle demanding and requiring a God who is sovereign. Among the meanings of sovereign as an adjective are the following: "supreme in power, superior to all others, supremely efficacious and effectual." God is all three of these in regard to His Word. He is supreme in His power in giving His Word, superior to all others in the glory of His Word, and supremely efficacious and effectual in guarding His Word. God is supreme above language—not limited by it but still using it. God is superior to all language changes—not diminished or damaged by them but able to override them. God is supremely efficacious and effectual above the processes of translation—not in bondage to either the human instruments of translation or the process itself but in control above them. God has not been caught weakhanded and flatfooted by the translation of Scripture from Hebrew, Aramaic and Greek into English. God did not fall prey to variant extant manuscripts of contradictory expression because translation posed such a difficulty for him. The variants are the work of the enemy, as the previous chapter shows. God is above all that. He is sovereignly omnipotent.

Simply stated, the inspiration and preservation of Scripture is on par with any other miracle God ever performed, including Creation. The heavens and earth which God spoke into existence out of nothing, and which "by the same word are kept in store...shall [one day] pass away with a great noise, and the elements shall melt with fervent heat, the earth also and the works that are therein shall be burned up" (II Peter 3:7, 10). No such passing away, melting and burning are ever connected with a demise, destruction and disappearance of God's Word.

Again, "Thou, Lord, in the beginning hast laid the foundation of the earth; and the heavens are the works of thine hands: They shall perish; but thou remainest; and they all shall wax old as doth a garment; And as a vesture shalt thou fold them up, and they shall be changed: but thou art the same, and thy years shall not fail...Therefore we ought to give the more earnest heed to the things which we have heard, lest at any time we should let them slip. For if the word spoken by angels was stedfast...How shall we escape, if we neglect so great salvation; which at the first began to be spoken by the Lord, and was confirmed unto us by them that heard him" (Hebrews 1:10–12; 2:1–3). These verses prove once again that the heavens and earth shall perish, but the unchanging God will remain. The permanence of the immutable God is strongly contrasted to the angels in Hebrews 1:13 and 14 (uncited above), and then that permanence is connected to the word spoken by God and confirmed to his apostles. No indication is given in the first two chapters of Hebrews that the Scriptures will ever perish or wax old like a worn garment. No indication is given in that passage that God ever folded up the Scriptures like a vesture. No word is written in those verses about the Scriptures changing. The passing of the heavens and earth and the positions of the angels are presented as temporary and subordinate in contrast to the permanence of the Scripture "spoken by the Lord, and…confirmed unto" the apostles.

Preservation of the Son and the Omnipotence of God. Certainly Christ suffered no loss of his perfections, even though God "made him to be sin for us…that we might be made the righteousness of God in him"; and He is thus "made unto us wisdom, and righteousness, and sanctification, and redemption" (II Corinthians 5:21; I Corinthians 1:30). He definitely maintained all His holy Godhead and Godhood despite having been "in all points tempted like as we are, yet without sin" (Hebrews 4:15). Christ endured no lessening of His holiness despite becoming our sin offering because God preserved him.

Any insistence that Jesus must have sinned stems from a belief in an impotent God who could not keep his sinless Son sinless. Any dogma that promotes a sinful Christ grows out of the fundamentally flawed notion that Jesus Christ, the only begotten of the Father, could not keep Himself above the temptations of Satan. Any belief system that teaches that Jesus Christ had sin and did sin must of necessity be grounded in the concept that the Holy Spirit could not fill Jesus Christ enough for Him not to sin.

Just because Jesus Christ was surrounded by sin does not mean that He sinned. He did not. Jesus Christ the Lord was preserved sinless, faultless and blameless throughout His earthly sojourn in spite of the onslaughts of the Devil, the blasphemy of the Pharisees, the ridicule of the Sadducees, the cruelty of the Romans, the rejection of the Jews, and the limitations of the flesh.

Preservation of the Saints and the Omnipotence of God. Again, God's oversight of His Word to ensure its intact availability to all generations is akin to His permanent saving and keeping of the individual souls of those who believe. Incidentally, it is not strange—or is it?—that those who insist that translation must, of necessity, produce errors also usually believe that sin in the believer's life must, of necessity, reproduce the lost condition. Their reasoning is that translation brings errors because God is impotent to oversee the work of men and prevent those errors; likewise, they assume that sin and iniquity condemn the believing soul because God is unable to override the believer's sin through the efficacious blood of His Son Jesus Christ.

Loss of biblical salvation once received is impossible. The atonement of Christ, his redemption and justification, his forgiveness and pardon, his reconciliation and redemption—all these marvelous provisions of salvation and more are permanent to the believing soul. "There is therefore now no condemnation to them which are in Christ Jesus, who walk not after the flesh, but after the Spirit" (Romans 8:1). "Verily, verily, I say unto you, He that heareth my word, and believeth on him that sent me, hath everlasting life, and shall not come into condemnation; but is passed from death unto life" (John 5:24).

True, the soul of any believer may entertain unseemly thoughts, erect ungainly strong holds and embrace many unholy behaviors; but the soul in grace remains in grace. Nothing is taken from God's perfect redemption by man's attitudes or actions in the flesh. God's miraculous salvation is not diminished one whit by the sins a man commits. Indeed, the soul of a believing sinner loses nothing of God's sanctified grace despite his committing sins, because God preserves him. The salvation he possesses in Jesus Christ is preserved in unassailable entirety and in absolute perfection.

Key in having faith to believe in a perfectly kept salvation is the remembrance that God is the Keeper, not the believer himself. Peter began his first epistle by ascribing a glorious praise to God who, "according to his abundant mercy hath begotten us again unto a lively hope by the resurrection of Jesus Christ from the dead, To an inheritance incorruptible, and undefiled, and that fadeth not away, reserved in heaven for you, Who are kept by the power of God through faith unto salvation ready to be revealed in the last time" (I Peter 1:3–5). Paul also attested to Pastor Titus of the abundant mercy of God that saved the soul in the first place when he wrote, "Not by works of righteousness which we have done, but according to his mercy he saved us, by the washing of regeneration, and renewing of the Holy Ghost; Which he shed on us abundantly through Jesus Christ our Saviour; That being justified by his grace, we should be made heirs according to the hope of eternal life" (Titus 3:5–7).

Peter's and Paul's words in these two portions alone are enough to keep the believer shouting "Glory!" for all the ages of eternity. The great and abundant mercy shed upon the sinner through Jesus Christ's sacrifice produces an effect. That effect, in Peter's words, is a lively hope through the merits and power of Jesus Christ's resurrection. Consequently, the believer has an inheritance reserved in Heaven. That inheritance is incorruptible by the flesh, undefiled by the world and cannot fade away even though Satan may attack and oppress. The reason for such protection is that God, by His power, keeps that saved soul through the faith of that saved soul to the day of a consummated salvation. The consummated salvation is the lively hope to which He has begotten that believer in the first place: the hope of receiving a resurrection body at the coming of Jesus Christ.

Paul further states that both the washing of regeneration and the renewing of the Holy Ghost play a part in the sinner's justification that makes him an heir, that is, the receiver of the inheritance of which Peter spoke. The washing of regeneration is the moment when the believing soul is first washed clean in the blood. The renewing of the Holy Ghost is the ongoing working of God in the life to keep that one within the grace of salvation. These two works of God do not trickle or sprinkle; they are shed abundantly into the life of a believing soul so that he can have the real hope of eternal life. What hope of eternal life can anyone have if he is in constant fear of losing the very life he gained at the moment of salvation? None at all. However, when Scripture is properly read and understood, that believer is soon singing the praises of the very God whose omnipotence does not allow Him to be impotent about keeping the saints saved!

Preservation of the Seed and the Omnipotence of God. Yet another miracle of sovereign oversight is God's supernatural initiation and preservation of the Jew through Isaac the promised seed and son of Abraham. Israel has endured as a people despite the Old Testament era's Hamans who sought to eradicate her from earthly existence. The earthly people of God have remained through the intertestamental era when they existed in spite of the effects of such truculent dictators as

Antiochus IV Epiphanes who sought their annihilation. The Jews have survived as a people even though the New Testament era's Islamic crusades and world-domination aspirants like Hitler and Stalin have attempted to obliterate her from the pages of history.

While it may be accurately argued that Abraham's descendents through Isaac have undergone many injuries, they yet remain. A Jew is still a Jew. An Israelite is still an Israelite. A Hebrew is still a Hebrew. They are still a people because God has preserved them through the millennia of time from the onslaughts of their ubiquitous enemies. What a miracle is the preservation of the Jewish bloodline, even in these end times wherein the loyalty of countries such as our own is in question! And we can be sure that God will preserve her all the way to the end, even in this violence-riddled twenty-first century when governments like Hamas and tyrants the likes of Iran's current leader are pontificating their intentions to destroy Israel.

No other nation has such a story of preservation. Egypt and Assyria, two mighty empires of the ancient world, have passed. The four world empires of Daniel's prophecy—the Babylonian, Medo-Persian, Greek, and Roman—no longer exist. Chronologically, they became lesser in glory but greater in strength, but even the mighty Romans have ceased. The Ottoman Empire of medieval history and the Holy Roman Empire of modern history are gone. Recent attempts at world dominion by Germany and Japan miserably failed. Today, these once-grand empires are either weakened nations or merely cities. Yes, they still exist, but they exist without having endured a *diaspora,* a worldwide dispersion.

The Jewish family is a miracle of God's preservation because she was continually barraged by enemies prior to her establishment in the Promised Land, constantly attacked by marauding would-be conquerors during her years in the land, eventually uprooted and exiled in Babylon, temporarily re-invested with nation status during the Restoration Era, and subsequently scattered throughout the entire world during the years after Malachi, the final voice among the prophets, wrote. Israel was not a recognized nation during the days of Christ and the apostles, nor had she been from the days of John, the last apostle, until 1948. However, she was still a people; and then, rising up from the ashes of the Gentiles' burnings, Israel came back upon the scene of nations. Today, Israel ranks once again among the most powerful countries on the entire world scene. Without delving into the singular details of her survival after having been scattered into every nation for well over two of the four millennia of her existence, this writer can authoritatively state that her preservation is certainly due to more than chance or her own strength. The survival of Israel is a preservationist's gold mine, a miracle-seeker's treasure trove! God in Heaven has had his hand upon "the apple of his eye" (Deuteronomy 32:10; Lamentations 2:18; Zechariah 2:8).

Another amazing fact with regard to the Jew is that during all their years of dispersion, their language has remained intact as well. All other integrated peoples of history eventually lost their own languages, and that situation did occur with some of the Jews (Nehemiah 13:24). However, God oversaw the maintenance of Hebrew as a language of spoken and written communication and preserved that language in such close proximity to its original form that Hebrew speakers and writers of today ably read and understand manuscripts that are dated well into the millennia before Christ! By contrast, Latin, the language of the Romans, is a dead language confined to the scrolls of antiquity and the pursuits of etymology.

Preservation of the Scripture and the Omnipotence of God. With acccuracy and perfection, the weeping prophet Jeremiah presents the student of Scripture one of the grandest revelations found anywhere in God's Word with regard to inspiration and preservation. God told Jeremiah, "Write...all the words that I have spoken unto thee against Israel, and against Judah, and against all the nations, from the day I spake unto thee, from the days of Josiah, even unto this day" (Jeremiah 36:2). Since Jeremiah's preaching ministry had commenced in the twelfth year of Josiah's thirty-one-year reign, and since Jehoahaz had reigned three months after the death of his father Josiah, and since this was the fourth year of Jehoiakim, it is no stretch to assume that God was commanding Jeremiah to write the words God had spoken to him over a period of almost a quarter century!

The process of this writing is described in Jeremiah 36:4: "Then Jeremiah called Baruch the son of Neriah: and Baruch wrote from the mouth of Jeremiah all the words of the LORD, which he had spoken unto him, upon a roll of a book." Again, note that the Holy Spirit says all the words were written, and it is here that the miracles of inspiration and preservation are given. Baruch *wrote* (past tense) all the words which God *had spoken* (past perfect tense), that is, the words that God had spoken to Jeremiah for nearly a quarter century. The use of the past perfect puts the past event of what was spoken to Jeremiah for some twenty-plus years prior to the past event of Baruch's writing.

The occasion of this inspiration-preservation miracle was during one of Jeremiah's imprisonments. God, ever a good user of time, directed his temporarily idled prophet to write down messages he had preached during the years of his ministry. He did not tell the prophet to write a synopsis or a summary of his life's messages. God did not command the prophet to pen the summative accumulation of thoughts that he had given to Jeremiah over that time period, but rather "all the words." This writing task was not an assignment given whereby the prophet was to recall to the best of his ability the gist of God's message; rather, he was to "write...all the words." Furthermore, Jeremiah was not given any allowance to write any other words, because God said, "Take thee a roll of a book, and write therein all the words that I have spoken unto thee." Any words that Jeremiah might have added would not have been words God had spoken.

In other words, one of two miracles took place. Either Jeremiah was able to recall in exact, word-for-word content the messages God had given him during his twenty-five-year ministry, or God superintended His prophet by inspiration. The latter is obvious. A simple comparison of Jeremiah 1:9, 36:4 and 36:18 demonstrates that God spoke to Jeremiah the definite words to speak in public and then later those same definite words to write in the roll of a book.

The purpose of God for this inspired and preserved writing was for Jeremiah to have Baruch write down those messages so that Baruch his scribe could then read them publicly (because Jeremiah was imprisoned). His hope was that a revival would occur, that Judah would repent and turn from their evil ways. The rebellious house of Judah had not repented when Jeremiah preached these messages from the mouth of God, but God chose to extend an additional opportunity through Baruch's reading of the inspired messages Jeremiah had preached over the course of a quarter-century. Baruch did this public reading on the feasting day "in the fifth year of Jehoiakim...in the ninth month" (vs. 9), a period of several months after God had given instruction for the writing in the fourth year of Jehoiakim. Several of Baruch's hearers, through a process of speaking to higher-ups, eventually relayed the truths of Jeremiah through Baruch to the king.

Upon hearing of Jeremiah's messages written out and read by Baruch, King Jehoiakim demanded that those writings be brought and read before him in his winter house. There, in his easy chair with slippered feet warmed by a crackling fire on his comfortable hearth, he sliced with his penknife one portion after another from the scroll and tossed those shreds of parchment into the fire as kindling "until all the roll was consumed in the fire that was on the hearth" (vs. 23). Gone, then, was the original, the inspired manuscript of that part of the Book of Jeremiah.

Upon this seemingly tragic turn of circumstances, God again spoke to Jeremiah and told him, "Take thee again another roll, and write in it all the former words that were in the first roll, which Jehoiakim the king of Judah hath burned" (vs. 28). Once again, the reader of Scripture is confronted with the fact that Jeremiah was expected to write every word. Nothing was to be added to what was in the first roll of what God had said. Nothing was to be subtracted from "all the former words." And indeed, without preservation of original inspiration, this instance would have been tragic indeed, but with the preservation oversight of an omnipotent God, the only tragedy was that of the hardening of the king's spirit against God.

The reader of Scripture is forced in this instance to assume that Jeremiah had a photographic memory with human recall of the many thousands of words which we now recognize as a major portion of the Book of Jeremiah or to believe in the miracle of preservation. Any thinking person is coerced to doubt sincerely the ability of any man (even a megasavant, and no evidence exists to suggest that Jeremiah was such a person) to recall verbatim thousands of words preached over a period of a quarter century and dictated one time. What is implicit and obvious is that by supernatural guidance of his prophet Jeremiah, there is a beautiful illustration of the preservation of Scripture. God preserved the record. Jeremiah procured "another roll, and gave it to Baruch the scribe...who wrote therein from the mouth of Jeremiah all the words of the book which Jehoiakim king of Judah had burned in the fire: and there were added besides unto them many like words" (vs. 32). The exact replication of the revelation plus the "many like words" (which we now recognize as the rest of the Book of Jeremiah) was possible, indeed simple, because God preserved His Word. God added the remainder of the prophecy, words of augmentaion and agreement, but certainly not words of dilution, doubt or denial of the previous revelation. What is miraculously amazing is that God preserved all of His Word to Jeremiah through the fire and back to the mouth of Jeremiah. From there that preserved word went into the ears and the pen of this faithful scribe so that "all the words" were saved.

One might argue that this occurred without the problem of translation. Such an argument is true. Both times, God gave the truth to Jeremiah in Hebrew. This argument would deal a serious death blow to the doctrine of preservation were it not so humorously and pathetically flawed. All one must do is consider which would be the grander miracle—the protection of God's Word through translation from one language to another with accurate manuscripts available or the complete reproduction of God's Word with only ashes available?

6

Does Translation Contaminate?

Proponents of the multiversional approach to bibliology generally insist that translation, of necessity, contaminates the message of the original as it passes to the second language of expression. Their claim is that, due to cultural differences and regional understandings, a certain dimension of meaning is changed or lost whenever translation takes place. According to this position, then, it is impossible to pass along a completely accurate message from one language to another.

Then, before the insanity of that boast has time to sink in, those same critics say, "A better translation would be…" or "A more accurately worded rendition would say…" What makes the translation of the multiversionist better or more accurately worded than the translation chosen by the King James translators? By what standard is the multiversionist's choice of words deemed better or more accurate than the word selected by the translators of the King James Bible? Certainly, few men living today have the linguistic training and qualifications that would parallel them with the King James translators. Therefore, it is evidently foundational that the multiversionist's choice of a "better word" is derived from reference to rare manuscripts, reliance upon their inferior intellect, and a rush to create a user-friendly, agenda-filled Bible.

It was Frances E. Willard who said, "He who sets his own copy keeps writing worse and worse." The multiversional approach abitrarily chooses which words need "improvement" and which ones do not based upon a few manuscripts that disagree with the majority and the individual multiversionist's whims and fancies.

The question remains. Does honest, well-studied, qualified translation corrupt or contaminate the original? Does the process of translation carried out by linguistically competent individuals result in a less-than-perfect rendition from the first language into the second? The answer is an emphatic and unequivocal "No." Within the confines of the Scripture itself, God has written His declarations about translation of languages when the only agenda in the translation is harmony with the exact definition, connotation and intention of the speaker.

Translation and the Origin of Languages. In the Word of God, the earliest mention of tongues and languages is found in Genesis chapters ten and eleven. Genesis 11:1 says, "And the whole earth was of one language, and of one speech." In short, everyone spoke the same language, and everyone understood one another. As in any large society, different dialects or pronunciations most surely existed. Probably colloquial expressions and local color within certain tribal groups created the need for a bit of adjustment if a person traveled far. However, much as a person with the familiar Boston accent can quickly acclimate and understand an individual from Atlanta or San Francisco and vice versa, so the people of the ancient cultures of the third millennium B.C. could communicate with one another without interpreters or translators.

Because the people of that time attempted to "build...a city and a tower, whose top may reach unto heaven; and...make...a name, lest [they] be scattered abroad upon the face of the whole earth...the Lord said, Behold, the people is one, and they have all one language; and this they begin to do: and now nothing will be restrained from them, which they have imagined to do. Go to, let us go down, and there confound their language, that they may not understand one another's speech" (Vss. 4, 6 and 7). God understood that pride in personal achievement and attainment was detrimental to mankind, so he miraculously created language barriers. For the first time in the history of man upon the created earth, different groups and tribes that had descended from Noah could not understand one another. People literally had to search in the mayhem that ensued to find people they understood. Those groups of souls who understood one another dispersed, as the Scripture says, "So the Lord scattered them abroad from thence upon the face of all the earth" (Genesis 11:8).

Once this had occurred, the only way for people of one language group to understand those of another language group was through a translator or interpreter. Genesis, the book of beginnings, is also the location of the earliest mention of people communicating through an interpreter. When Joseph's brothers first came to Egypt to buy corn because of the extremity of intense famine, "Joseph saw his brethren...and Joseph knew his brethren, but they knew not him...and they knew not that Joseph understood them; for he spake unto them by an interpreter" (Genesis 42:7, 8, and 23). Joseph, wanting to test his brothers, concealed his identity and "made himself strange unto them, and spake roughly unto them" (Vs. 7). His only communicating with his brothers was in the Egyptian language through a bilingual interpreter who knew both Hebrew and Egyptian.

As an aside, the court of Pharaoh must have employed many such bi- or multi-lingual interpreters who were familiar with languages from the surrounding lands, because "all countries came into Egypt to Joseph for to buy corn; because that the famine was so sore in all lands" (41:57). The interpreter through whom Joseph conversed with his brothers was one of perhaps twenty or thirty so employed in the royal courts of the largest empire of that day.

The content of the conversation that Joseph and his brothers had through the interpreter on that first visit is recorded in Genesis 42:7–20. Basically, Joseph asked them of their purpose, and they told him they had come for food. Joseph responded with an accusation that they were spies, and they denied that, asserting that they were the noble sons of one man in need of food. When Joseph refused this explanation, one of the ten brothers spoke up and told the story of Jacob and his twelve sons, mentioning that the youngest (Benjamin) was at home with his father, that one was "not," and that the other ten were present. Joseph devised a plan to prove his brothers, a plan that involved one of the brothers returning to Jacob to fetch Benjamin while the others remained in captivity in Egypt. Then, because Joseph feared God, he reduced the count from nine to one, requiring that only one remain behind in prison while the other nine returned to Jacob. Verse twenty-four mentions that Joseph communed further with his brothers, but no details of that portion of the conversation are given.

When Joseph's nine brothers returned to Jacob in the land of Canaan, they told the story to their father. Their rendition of the story in Genesis 42:30–34 indicates that they had no problem understanding what Joseph's demands were, spoken in Egyptian but translated into Hebrew through an interpreter. Jacob's response in Genesis 42:36–38 further proves that Jacob had no difficulty comprehending what the nine brothers related of Joseph's Egyptian message. The point is that nothing was lost when the interpreter communicated Joseph's Egyptian speech to the ten brothers in Hebrew. Nothing was lost when the ten brothers communicated through the interpreter back to Joseph. Neither was anything added, making the message different or inaccurate. Neither was anything twisted, perverted, misunderstood, or left in question.

In Genesis 43, when Jacob deemed it necessary to send his nine sons for more corn, the full weight of Joseph's demands brought about Jacob's resignation to allow Benjamin to travel. Why did this happen? Simple. They all understood perfectly what they had heard through an interpreter in Pharaoh's court because Pharaoh's interpreters were qualified men who were trained to relay accurate messages.

Another situation that occurred far later in Bible history gives additional irrefutable proof of the ability for people accurately to understand and use more than one language interchangeably. King Hezekiah and the people of Judah were beseiged by King Sennacharib and the army of Assyria. Sennacharib sent his henchman Rabshakeh to Jerusalem with threatening messages designed to humiliate and undermine Hezekiah. As Rabshakeh spewed forth words of blasphemy against God and ridicule against Hezekiah, three of Hezekiah's chief servants—Eliakim, Shebna, and Joah—interrupted him and said, "Speak, I pray thee, unto thy servants in the Syrian language; for we understand it: and speak not to us in the Jews' language, in the ears of the people that are on the wall" (Isaiah 36:11).

Eliakim was over Hezekiah's house and had charge of the safety of the king and his family. Shebna was the royal scribe, charged with copying edicts and writing out official messages. Joah was the recorder, employed to write down the conversations about affairs of state for future reference. These three witnesses stood on the wall and requested that Rabshakeh converse with them in another language which they could understand and use, but which the commoners could not. This would accomplish two things. The officials would understand Sennacherib's sinister curses and seditious cruelty, but the citizenry would not be discouraged or frightened.

What this means is that Hezekiah's men could understand both languages and translate from one to the other without losing, changing or gaining any meaning. Hezekiah's men could hear either language, translate from either one into the other and understand both without violation of the message. This further means that Rabshakeh, who obviously received the message from Sennacherib in the Syrian language, was able to hear, translate and speak in either language. On pain of death, he was required to deliver an accurate message. He could not have returned to Sennacherib having delivered an inexact message. What he said in Hebrew at the wall of Jerusalem was precisely what Sennacherib had told him in Syrian before he left Lachish (Vs. 2).

The importance of recounting the details of Babel and the confusion of the languages, of Joseph and his interpreter, and of the bilingual servants of Hezekiah's and Sennacherib's courts is obvious. Even though mankind had been scattered over the world and separated into language groups because of barriers, man learned ways to cross those boundaries through accurate translators. Obviously, God must have foreseen such people employed to communicate language. Furthermore, he must have known that those people would be able to communicate accurately. If God had not, from Genesis chapter eleven forward, planned to use the work of faithful translators, His confounding of languages essentially doomed all language groups except the one receiving his original revelation to life without truth and death without hope. Such predestination of helpless souls to truthless, hopeless existence may well be Calvinistic, but it is neither Christian nor biblical.

Translation of the Gospel Message. The events of the Day of Pentecost provide the student of Scripture with unassailable proof that proper translation can and does communicate a truth identical with original wording. The true gift of tongues—not the charismatic misuse through gibberish and unintelligible spoofery but the Pentecostal power that accompanied the coming of the Holy Spirit—resulted in a translation miracle whereby not fewer than a dozen language groups heard the exact same message! "And when the day of Pentecost was fully come...they were all filled with the Holy Ghost, and began to speak with other tongues, as the Spirit gave them utterance. And...every man heard them speak in his own language. And they were all amazed and marvelled, saying...how hear we every man in our own tongue, wherein we were born?...we do hear them speak in our tongues the wonderful works of God" (Acts 2:1–11).

Pentecost and its gospelizing of the people groups present in Jerusalem for the big annual feast time demonstrates that the act of translating from one language to another does not automatically cause meaning and value from the first language to be lost due to the confines of the second language. Neither does the work of translating from the original to a second tongue automatically result in adding nuance or innuendo from the first tongue to the second. Furthermore, the task of translating from the first to the second language does not automatically force a twisting or a thwarting of the message as the translation occurs.

If indeed such diminishing or adding or changing must of necessity have taken place on the Day of Pentecost, only one language group could have heard the true Gospel, and all the other people groups must have heard a gospel that was contaminated or lessened or mutilated in some way due to the cultural limitations of language and the cultural understanding of both the speaker and the hearers. If that were true, many of the thousands of souls, whom Peter addressed after he stood up with the other eleven, heard a gospel message that was somehow imprecise and unreliable.

Comparison with the Holy Ghost's lambasting of "another gospel: Which is not another" (Galatians 1:6,7) conclusively verifies that, if that Gospel of the grace of God preached from the lips of Peter and the eleven had been diluted or polluted as it passed from Greek to those many other languages, they would have been blessed in communicating to all Greek hearers but accursed for preaching a false gospel to all the other hearers. Such an enigma presents the Holy Spirit as a communicator of contradictory messages, a blasphemous impossibility given the character of "God, that cannot lie" (Titus 1:2).

Another obvious outcome, if the gospel preached by twelve Galileans on that day changed as it passed from the Greek language to the tongues of the dozen or more national groups present at Jerusalem, is that the hearers would never have been saved because salvation is not possible without the true Gospel. That means that any among those who "gladly received his word" and "were baptized" and "were added unto them" (Acts 2:41) who did not speak the language of Peter were false converts, doomed to the deception of having been unable to receive the true Gospel because of the language barrier!

Nothing in the Book of Acts or in any other book of the Bible indicates that any among the three thousand converts on that day were false professors. In fact, Luke later cites the Pentecost converts as true believers, indeed as the acid test whereby the saving faith of others was judged. Luke's account of Peter's message at the house of Gentile Cornelius states that "the Holy Ghost fell on all them which heard the word…[and since] God gave them the like gift as he did unto us, who believed on the Lord Jesus Christ; what was I, that I could withstand God? When they heard these things, they held their peace, and glorified God, saying, Then hath God also to the Gentiles granted repentance unto life" (10:44;11:17 and 18).

In conclusion, the redemptive Gospel of the grace of Jesus Christ, necessary for salvation, suffered no pejoration as it was spoken on Pentecost in one language by the Galilean preachers and was translated from their mouths into over a dozen languages. The justifying Gospel of the grace of Jesus Christ experienced no improvements as it proceeded through the air from the Greek tongue to the tongues of those in the audience. Every person heard the exact same message, and all those who were saved were saved by the exact same Gospel.

Translation of Names. In another Holy-Ghost-inspired example of translation, God said, "They shall call his name Emmanuel, which being interpreted is, God with us" (Matthew 1:23). First, it is important to note that the word *interpreted* obviously carries the meaning "translated." The Hebrew name from Isaiah's prophecy was translated into Matthew's Greek and has since been translated into King James' English. Did the Hebrew meaning of God's name lose something or gain something or change by being translated into the words *God with us*? Was God's name contaminated or diminished or added to because God took it from one language and expressed it in another? Does the Hebrew mind that says Emmanuel understand something different than the Greek mind or the English mind that says God with us? No and no and no. Nothing is lost, gained or changed by the expression of the Hebrew into the English. The meaning is the same. The words are identical in expression, connotation and definition.

John the apostle recorded another account of translation of names that demonstrably supplements the argument that translation can occur without the sacrifice of accuracy. When Jesus was conversing with the Samaritan woman at Jacob's well, "the woman saith unto him, I know that Messias cometh, which is called Christ: when he is come, he will tell us all things" (John 4:25). Who is he? Is he Messiah or Christ? Was some spiritual or eternal quality of the Messiah diminished or squandered by the woman's translation of the Hebrew *Messias* to the Greek *Christos?* Did this woman inadvertently, or even purposely, add to the perfection of the Hebrew *Messiah* by equating him to the Greek *Christ?*

Apparently Jesus Himself did not think so, because He immediately responded, "I that speak unto thee am he" (Vs. 26). Jesus' use of the word *he* grammatically proves that what the Hebrew understood when he said or heard *Messias* and what the Greek understood when he said or heard *Christos* were identical. Were *Messiah* and *Christ* not identical, Jesus would have to have said, "I that speak unto thee am both," "I that speak unto thee am Messiah," or "I that speak unto thee am Christ." By saying *he,* the Lord made the Hebrew title *Messias* the express image of the Greek title *Christos,* not merely the dynamic equivalent or the closest approximation of it.

Another detail that is weighty indeed with regard to the words of the Samaritan woman at the well is that, even as a lost person without any spiritual insight, she accurately translated a word from one language to another. This does not mean that this writer supports the concept of unregenerate souls translating Scripture; rather, it illustrates that regardless of whether or not a person is saved, a word means what a word means. The lost woman knew enough Hebrew and Greek to know that the two words, Messias and Christos, were exact replicas, mirror images if you please, of each other. She was not perverting or improving or changing anything. She had no agenda to do so, and she stood to receive no benefit had she done so. She was simply expressing in what the Holy Ghost would later add to His inspired record that translation does not hinder meaning when translation is done correctly.

Several translations of names are given in both the Old and New Testaments. As God moved in the life of the patriarch Abram, he provided an unanswerable apologetic with regard to the accuracy possible in the work of translation. God said, "Neither shall thy name any more be called Abram, but thy name shall be Abraham; for a father of many nations have I made thee" (Genesis 17:5). Nearly nineteen hundred years—and many copyists—later, Paul cited that statement and wrote, "Abraham; who is the father of us all; (As it is written, I have made thee a father of many nations,)" (Romans 4:16, 17). God translated the name *Abraham* into its literal meaning in Hebrew and said that the name meant "father of many nations." Then, he translated the name *Abraham* into its exact Greek meaning and said that the name meant "father of many nations." What was lost or gained by the translation? What was left out or added? changed? diluted or polluted? misunderstood? relegated to inaccuracy? responsible for confusion? Nothing. And what was lost or gained or changed or misunderstood because the King James translators expressed Abraham's name and its meaning in the English language? Nothing. Translation, when it is performed in spiritual light with clear conscience and for good faith, communicates in the second language exactly what it communicated in the first.

Scripture testifies to the accuracy of translation from the mouth of God to the pens of men, from the Hebrew language to the Greek, from the pen of the prophet to the pen of the apostle, from the lips of the lost to the ears of the Lord, and from the faithful text to the faithful translations.

In conclusion, perhaps, a couple of mundane but accurate extrabiblical illustrations could add a bit of light to this subject as well. In math class, students learn to write equations (called word sentences) such as $2 + 2 = 4$. In that elemetary expression, a translation occurs. The first language is $2 + 2$; the second language is 4. In any culture in any land in any age, a person with precious little education or training understands that if a person says $2 + 2$ or if he says 4, he means the exact same thing. They are equal, even though they do not sound or look the same.

When a child enrolls in a music class, he begins quite soon to learn notes. As he progresses, he comes to realize that A-flat and G-sharp are the exact same key on whatever instrument he is playing; furthermore, he comes to see that they are the exact same tone regardless of the key signature of the musical composition he is studying. While this writer is untrained with regard to music theory, he knows enough to state that in one key signature that black key on the piano is called A-flat but in another it is referred to as G-sharp, even though it is the exact same key. A translation from one key to another can occur without changing the sound or value of that note. Whether the G is sharped or the A flatted, the tone is identical. Translation, whether in math or music or the Scripture itself, is accurate when done with precision.

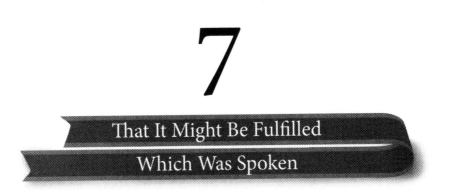

7

That It Might Be Fulfilled

Which Was Spoken

Fulfilled prophecy is one of the mightiest and most concrete of all arguments in favor of inspiration and preservation in all of Christian experience. The amazing accuracy with which past prophecies have been fulfilled and are being fulfilled even at this hour gives credibility to the preservation of an inspired message from God.

The spiritual logic of this position is as follows: The specific wording of a prophecy relates to its inspiration, and the exactness of a fulfillment relates to preservation. If a prophecy were not inspired, no one would expect its fulfillment or be able to tell if it had been fulfilled; if the prophecy were not preserved, no one living beyond the generation in which the prophecy was originally given could be aware that a particular prophecy awaited fulfillment.

If the Scripture were inspired in its original languages but only to its original recipients, the nonpreservation of the Scripture would render all prophecy suspect as soon as it was first handed down or first translated. By virtue of the non-preservationist position, any prophecy becomes flawed once it survives beyond the time of its original pronouncement. What such a position fosters is doubt rather than faith and questions rather than answers.

The support base upon which the Gospel of Matthew rests is the phrase "that it might be fulfilled which was spoken by the prophet, saying...." God's purpose in giving Matthew a Gospel was to give the Jews a message that they would have difficulty rejecting. One thing common to orthodox Jews is a respect for the Old Testament Scriptures. The exacting care with which the orthodox scribes copied the words of the prophets is documented testimony to their awe and admiration of the Old Testament. Matthew was inspired to make nearly twenty specific references to prophecies that were fulfilled in either the life or death experiences of the God-Man Jesus Christ. The power of such references is that those prophecies still existed in exact, preserved form and the Jews knew of those exact, preserved prophecies. When they were fulfilled in precise detail as they were given, they pointed the Jewish unbelieving mind toward the Messiah. Had those prophecies been corrupted by translation or by the fluid changes in language which occur over hundreds of years, Matthew would not have been able to refer to them, because their form and message would no longer have been recognizable to later generations.

Isaiah's grand fifty-third chapter and David's graphic twenty-second psalm are far more than approximate and temporary descriptions of the offering up of the Son of God for sinners. They are inspired, preserved accounts of death by crucifixion. What makes those accounts even more valuable is that crucifixion was a means of death invented after the writings of David and Isaiah! Certainly there was time before the crucifixion of Christ centuries later for the language to change and the dialects to differ and the spellings to vary to the point that man could have easily altered the prophecies of David and Isaiah concerning crucifixion until they were unrecognizable. However, those prophecies were preserved throughout those centuries so that when Matthew wrote his Gospel, there was substance to his citations of fulfillment.

Which of us has not heard or read a marvelous message based upon the gloriously and technically accurate prophecies and the marvelously and specifically pertinent fulfillments of Calvary? None of those messages could have had any real merit had not the Lord personally overseen and preserved those texts for the centries prior to Christ and for the two millennia that have passed since He died and rose again. Preachers, evangelists and soul winners would not be able to refer to these portions and their fulfillments in the Gospels authoritatively to describe the intense sufferings of our Saviour for the sins of mankind if the content of those texts were suspect.

John the son of Zebedee and beloved apostle of Jesus Christ illustrated this point with clarity. As the triumphal entry of Christ into Jerusalem got under way, the people took palm branches and strewed them in the streets where Jesus would be riding. Christ himself, riding upon a young ass, came into the city to the hosannas of the children and the blessings of the adults. Luke reported that as Christ rode past the multitudes who were rejoicing, the Pharisees called upon Him to rebuke His disciples. To this Jesus replied that if the disciples held their peace, the rocks would cry out. John then gave the detail that "these things understood not his disciples at the first: but when Jesus was glorified, then remembered they that these things were written of him, and that they had done these things unto him" (John 12:16).

The prophecy of these things that "were written of him" is found in Zechariah 9:9, written by the prophet during the Restoration over five centuries earlier than John wrote. During those five-plus centuries, Israel had existed, as historians are wont to say, "between the anvil and the hammer." Syria to the north and Egypt to the south had repeatedly met in battle in the Holy Land of Israel, but during all that social turmoil and military unrest, the prophecy survived. During all the migrations of the Jews out of the Holy Land as they fled for their very lives, the manuscripts lived without having been destroyed. By the time of Christ, Roman imperial government had ensured peace—the now-famous *Pax Romana*—so that Jews living in the Holy Land were safe. Into this time period Christ was born and grew up. He entered His public ministry and engaged in preaching, teaching, discipling, healing, and cleansing. Near the conclusion of this earthly work, the incident of the palm branches and of Christ's riding into Jerusalem on a donkey to the music of the hosannas and praises took place. Christ then died and rose again and ascended. At some time after all that, the disciples were conversing, and the events of the triumphal entry came up. One of the disciples brought up the fact that Zechariah had prophesied the events that happened on that day as Christ rode into Jerusalem.

Those disciples could never have remembered "that these things were written of him" if the things written of Him had been destroyed, altered, reworded, or otherwise marred. If the things written by Zechariah in the earliest part of the fifth century B.C. had undergone even as many changes in five centuries as the so-called Scriptures have undergone in the last fifty years, the message of Zechariah would have been unrecognizable, and no disciple, however studious, could have known that such things were written.

In addition, it is notable that the inspiration of any prophecy in its original and the subsequent preservation of that same prophecy eliminate the possibility of coincidence or accident in the fulfillment. Any intellectually honest person must agree that the hundreds of Scripture prophecies already fulfilled in exact detail defy the odds of coincidence! Any intellectually honest person must also agree that those same fulfillments are the foreseen result of an Intelligent Designer, not the accidental occurrence of the explosion of world events.

Again, the same intellectually honest individual must agree that the specific accuracy with which prophecies have been fulfilled and are being fulfilled defies any possible conspiracy theory. No man could have possibly planned a conspiracy for the fulfillment of a fairy tale with so many prophecies from so many different people about so many other different people and events from so many different time periods. Prophecies discovered within the pages of Scripture are the spoken and guarded Word of the living God. No other explanation will even come close to satisfying the investigative prowess of any honest-minded seeker of truth.

Doubting the inspiration and preservation of Scripture is turning the miraculous into the mythical and converting amazement into mockery. This is just what the multiversion, nonpreservationist crowd is bringing to pass, forcing those of us who still believe the Bible to go soul winning into cities and towns where the vast majority of those we meet don't believe the Bible is reliable. A Gospel that saves sinners, when read out of an unreliable Bible, gets scoffed at. A Gospel that guarantees Heaven, when read out of a mistake-laden Bible, gets derided. Follow-up visits and discipleship efforts are equally daunting because a Scripture that requires submission and obedience is immediately pushed aside by new believers who have heard all their lives about "the errors" in the Bible. Even well-seasoned believers are affected; more and more, pastors and evangelists and teachers in the church face the questioning looks of those in the pew when "Thus saith the Lord" is read from the pulpit.

Thus the importance of prophecy as it relates to inspiration and preservation is established. Those believing in a perfect Scripture have the joy of trusting in things to come because they believe in things that have come. Those who trust in an unmarred, infallible Bible look forward to the fulfillment of exact prophecies because they look back on the fulfillments of others. The remainder of this chapter, therefore, will treat two main types of prophecy and show the power of fulfillments.

Prophecy seems to be categorized under two main headings. One of those main strains of Bible prophecy concerns the sequence of world empires and the rise and fall of nations in the history of the world. A second type of prohecy deals with specific people—our Lord Jesus Christ primarily and other individuals on a lesser scale. The detail with which prophecies were fulfilled speaks not only of the inspired accuracy of the original prophetic utterance but also of its preservation throughout centuries until its fulfillment. Were the prophecies not preserved, but lost or marred, then even if fulfillment occurred, no one would recognize the fulfillment.

Empires and Nations of World History. The bulk of prophecy regarding nations is about the nation of Israel. Beginning in Genesis chapter twelve, God devotes thirty-nine books of Old Testament revelation to the unfolding of the history of his chosen, covenant people. Minute prophetic detail is devoted to Israel with regard to the borders of the nation, the establishment of the nation within those borders, the kings who would rule in that nation, the wars that would be fought by the nation, the idolatry that would destroy that nation, the troubles that would befall the nation, the captivity of the nation by Assyria and Babylon, the restoration of the nation under Medo-Persian authority, the dispersion of the nation for thousands of years, the regathering of the nation in the last days, the final attack against the nation at Armageddon, the deliverance of the nation at the end of the Tribulation, and the millennial reign of Christ within the borders of that nation.

Of the prophecies regarding Israel, many have already seen their fulfillment; others await fulfillment. Statements about the earthly covenant people of God made by Moses as long ago as fifteen centuries before Christ were fulfilled with such perfect conformity to the original as to prove the miraculous preservation of those originals. Other statements about Israel were made at various times during the ensuing fifteen centuries, and again, the fulfillments were so exact as to defy happenstance and prove the preservation of the originals. Still other predictions made by Christ and the apostles in the first century A.D. have come to pass with clockwork precision, again proving the preservation of the words first spoken.

Leaders and People of World History. Most of the prophecy in Scripture dealing with individuals concerns the Messiah, the Lord Jesus Christ; but some of it is focused upon others.

Consider the amazing detail of the prophecy of the unnamed man of God in I Kings 13:1–3 and its down-to-the-detail fulfillment in II Kings 23:10–20. The events of I Kings 13 took place around 945 B.C., while II Kings 23 occurred in about 623 B.C. The lapse of some three hundred twenty years was not too long, however, for God to oversee the fulfillment of such cardinal points as Josiah's name, bloodline and specific actions with regard to idols and statues! What if those details had been blurred by language changes? What if those minutiae had been omitted? What if a scribe had carelessly copied a different name? carelessly named a different bloodline? carelessly added certain actions? Had such things occurred, no reader would marvel at II Kings 23; that chapter would have been a simple recording of events. However, when those events which might seem trivial without a precursive prophecy are seen in light of that original prophecy, they are no longer trivial! They become enormous, prominent and consequential. And they add to the proof of the preservation of Scripture.

The inspired words of Elijah to Ahab in I Kings 21 are particular in their detail. God told Ahab in that original message that dogs would lick his blood in the same place where they licked the blood of Naboth, that his seed would die out like the seed of Jeroboam died out, that Jezebel would die by the ramparts of Jezreel, that dogs would eat Jezebel at her death, and that his children's deaths would be gruesome and dishonourable. Part of the fulfillment of these amazingly detailed prophecies came in I Kings 22:37, 38 at the death of Ahab just about three years after their original inspiration. Other parts of their fulfillment came more than two decades later when Jehu executed the Lord's vengeance upon Jezebel and the seed of Ahab. Second Kings 9:25, 26;

9:36, 37; and 10:30 give the exact details of the fulfillments. Jehu said, "This is the word of the Lord, which he spake by his servant Elijah the Tishbite." What Jehu was saying is that Elijah's words, written down some two decades prior, had not been changed or altered, but that they had been preserved so that at their fulfillment they were recognized as accurate by all who knew the original prophecy.

Another marvelous example of fulfilled prophecy came to King Jehu in II Kings 10:30 when the Lord promised Jehu four generations to sit upon the throne of Israel because of his obedience in destroying Baal worship and Ahab's seed. Chronologers place the date of that prophecy around 855 B.C. The final fulfillment of that prophecy came some ninety-three years later in 762 B.C. as recorded in II Kings 15:12. What brilliance on the part of God to have the prophet write in the original inspired prophecy about Jehu's "children of the fourth generation" and then to have him write in the final fulfillment the words "unto the fourth generation." How easily a careless scribe could have changed the words slightly to annul the prophecy! How quickly an astute reader could have discerned the contradiction if those words had not been preserved! But they were, and they are.

For all these prophecies and their amazing accuracy, they pale in comparison to the exact prophecies and exact fulfillments with regard to the Messiah, the Lord Jesus Christ. Many of the prophecies of Christ were made over a thousand years before His birth by such prophets as Job, Moses and Samuel. Others were made in the millennium before His birth by such holy men of God as David, Isaiah, Daniel, Micah, Haggai, and Malachi to name a few. Mathematicians in the field of probability have calculated that for all the actual prophecies of Christ to have come to their perfect fulfillment in one man would require odds of an impossible degree. It is for such reasons as this that liberal scholars are so avidly seeking to destroy the accurate record of the King James Bible by casting doubt on the actual authorship of certain books of the Bible, on the accepted dates of prophetic writings and on the entire concept of the preservation of Scripture.

The lineage of the Lord through Abraham, Isaac, Jacob, Judah, and David is prophesied in Genesis and II Samuel, with undeniable fulfillment in Matthew and Luke. The virgin birth of our Saviour is prophesied in Isaiah and specifically fulfilled in Matthew. The birth of the Lord Jesus Christ is prophesied in Micah as occurring in Bethlehem with exact fulfillment recorded in Luke. The prophecy of a forerunner, John the Baptist, is given in Isaiah and Malachi with irrefutable fulfillment in the Gospels. Isaiah and the psalmist gave specific revelation with regard to the content and manner of the Messiah's teaching as well as to His miracles of healing. These prophecies are fulfilled in exactitude in all four Gospels and alluded to in Acts, Romans and Hebrews. The triumphal entry already cited in this chapter was inspired in Zechariah and fulfilled in all four gospel accounts. The timing of the coming of the Messiah is given in Daniel's prophecy and fulfilled in the Gospels.

As to the details of Christ's crucifixion, the list is amazing. Psalm 22 outlines the nakedness, the mockery, the gambling for his garments, the darkness, the great cry, and the broken heart. His pierced side is prophesied by Zechariah; the vinegar is spoken of in Psalm 69. Isaiah chapters 50–53 mention the smiting of Christ's back, the pulling out of handfuls of hair, the beatings and bruisings of the Saviour's body, the silence of the Christ at His trial, the thieves who were His companions at His death, His burial in a rich man's grave, His travail, His offering for sin, and His resurrection. All these and more are fulfilled exactly in the gospel accounts. The resurrection of the Lord Jesus Christ— adamantly taught in its precise fulfillment in all four Gospels, the Book of Acts and in nearly every New Testament Epistle—finds its prophetic roots in the writings of Job, David, Hosea, Isaiah, and others.

How important it is to the subjects of inspiration and preservation that both the record of any given prophecy and the record of its fulfillment agree! Minor word changes to any given prophecy or fulfillment could render the prophecy unfulfilled, and thus render the Scripture seemingly inaccurate. If, as the multiversionists promote, the dozens of scribal errors really do exist, all prophecy and all fulfillment are in question. If prophecy and fulfillment are indeed in question, we who have hope in Christ have no substantive hope at all but only a mirage on the horizons of our earthly deserts.

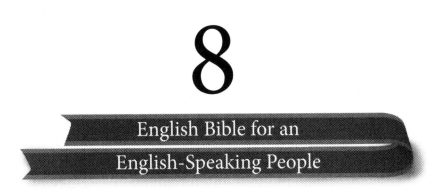

8

English Bible for an English-Speaking People

Ancient landmarks of the Baptists who have lived in every generation since Pentecost have included the belief that the Word of God should be available in the language of the common people, not to the point of its condescension to engage corrupt minds and licentious cultures, but always to the extent that any seeking soul might have access to God's eternal truths. To ensure this privilege, many Baptists, and indeed, many Bible-believing, Bible-loving people from a variety of other groups have given their lives in the cause of Bible publication and Bible distribution.

Prominent in the history of man has been the constant effort to keep the Scriptures away from the common people. A part of the Devil's program in every age has been to wrest the Scriptures away from the man at his profession, away from the woman in her home, and away from the child in the sandlot. Having over time deprived the bulk of any given society of the privilege of Scripture availability, Satan has then established a religious system that is always based in one dimension or another on the fact that the deep mysteries of the Bible are discernible only by the educated elite and the faithful few of a religious hierarchy.

One of the most recent cultures to have been founded is that of the United States. Upon the establishment of this infant nation, many of our founding fathers avowed the significance of having Scripture available to the people. Whether it be the modern-day United States of America or medieval England or any other place in any other time, "the good fight of faith" (I Timothy 6:12) has included the effort—at times at the forefront and at times in the background—to keep the Scriptures available to the masses so that no such gap can develop between the average believer (or unbeliever for that matter) and the pseudointellectuals who believe they have exclusive rights, duties and abilities to explain the Scriptures.

Preachers and teachers who purport that only those who have a grasp on Greek and Hebrew can truly understand the Bible are, in essence, severing the masses of worshipers in any given Bible-believing church on any given Sunday (and even a large majority of their pastors and staff) from the established elite who have a working knowledge of the languages of the original manuscripts of the Old and New Testaments.

If the only people within our English-speaking culture who really know God's message are those scholars who can read and understand the Hebrew Masoretic Text and the Greek *Textus Receptus,* then a full ninety-nine percent of Christians in the English-speaking world are out of the loop in comprehending God's message or will for their lives. However, the scholars who can read and understand Hebrew and Greek do not possess exclusive understanding of God's Word and will. The King James Bible is an English Bible for English-speaking people. Due to that fact, English-speaking individuals can comprehend God's message, methods, manner, and mandates by reading the King James Engish Bible.

This is not a denial of the *value of familiarity* with the Hebrew and Greek languages for confirmation of God's truth; rather, it is a denial of the *necessity of such a familiarity* with the Hebrew and Greek languages for comprehension of that truth. Any position that mocks or unduly criticizes the original languages is ignorant, but equally ignorant is the position that the English Bible cannot be comprehended without consultation with Greek and Hebrew. The merit of the original languages is not in the progressive discovery of God's Word by higher critics of our technologically advanced but spiritually stunted society. No. The value of the original languages is that holy commoners in sanctified homes and separated churches and schools can consult them and find that the King James Bible is perfectly rendered, accurately translated and beautifully preserved!

If it be true that Hebrew and Greek proficiency are necessary for the proper understanding of our English King James Bible, then we who are Baptists—indeed fundamentalists, inspirationists and preservationists—are guilty of establishing a clergy-laity gap on a par with Roman Catholicism. If only the privileged who study and know Hebrew and Greek can get the "full meaning" of Scripture, the result will be the separating of pastors from their congregations and of teachers from their classes.

Whether these fundamentalists are consciously or unconsciously engaged in this exercise is not for man to judge, for we are to "judge nothing before the time, until the Lord come, who both will bring to light the hidden things of darkness, and will make manifest the counsels of the hearts"(I Corinthians 4:5). As a mere man without access to the invisible, this writer must beg ignorance with regard to the reasons and motives that fundamentalists might insist that Hebrew and Greek must be understood if the Scripture is to be "truly meaningful" or "fully comprehended" or "properly applied."

This author yearns to believe that the majority of those fundamentalists who are promoting this position are doing so without having thoroughly considered the ultimate outcome of the concept. However, judicious evaluation leads this author to aver almost certainly that there are fundamentalists who have adequately weighed their position and who knowingly preach to their congregations and teach in their classrooms that no man can be "a workman that needeth not to be ashamed, rightly dividing the word of truth" (II Timothy 2:15) unless he knows the original languages! Having so preached or taught, such a spokesman has elevated himself to a pinnacle he does not deserve and has relegated most, if not all, of his hearers to the position of not only not knowing the Scriptures but also of *not being able* to know the Scriptures!

God has most assuredly inspired and preserved His Word to man. That said, let it be just as assuredly understood that in His miraculous preservation of His Word for generations and centuries and millennia, He has not been caught off guard by that fact that, with the passing of those centuries and millennia, languages have been unpredictable. God has not been surprised that some languages that once were used both for commerce and for conversation (such as Latin) have disappeared and are no longer used for either one. Nor has the Lord been shocked by the development of a new language that was not in use or even in its infancy (such as English) when the autographs were written. Furthermore, God has not been blindsided by the fact that some languages have remained in existence and usage over the millennia but in those millennia have undergone substantial changes.

God's supernatural supervision of copies within a language and of translations from one language to another did not require a separate act of inspiration for every copy or translation. Rather, the same God whose power could be superimposed upon the original writers of Scripture in the miraculous work of inspiration also overshadowed holy men generations and centuries later as they copied and translated. In this distinct work, God did not "re-inspire" Scripture but simply preserved the inspiration already inherent in His revelation. This marvelous evidence of God's power can be explained simply. Just as God comes to indwell a believer at the moment when a sinner repents toward God and receives faith toward our Lord Jesus Christ, so God inspired His Word in the original. Then, just as that indwelling Spirit stays within that man forever, so God stays in His Word forever. And like the indwelling Spirit fills a believer from time to time to do His bidding, so God's Spirit, from time to time, has come upon His Word to oversee its transmission from one copy to another and its translation from one language to another.

Notably, Jude called attention to "the faith which was once delivered unto the saints" (Vs. 3). He did not refer to any second delivery or tenth delivery that would have occurred in the ensuing centuries if "re-inspiration" were God's means. The faith, that is, the total embodiment of God's word-for-word truth, was delivered once by inspiration and preservation, and that preservation has guaranteed the veracity of millions of careful copies and many true translations into languages other than the originals. The King James Bible, one such translation that has come to the world, is inspired and preserved in English. It needs no improvements or corrections! It is God's pure, infallible, immutable, impeccable, miraculous Word!

The entire thrust of Jude's mention of the faith once delivered was that the faithful were to "earnestly contend" for that faith. Why? Simple. The Devil would ever be earnestly contending against it! And one of the ways the Devil earnestly contends against it is to confuse the issues of translation to persuade people that translation must, of necessity, somehow taint or tamper with the truth. Undeniably, many of the perverted translations that have been derived from unreliable manuscripts are tainted. However, the translation is not tainted because it is a translation but because the manuscript from which it was translated is tainted. In such translations, the message thus tampered with in the original remains inaccurate in the translation as well. But in the faithful translation by translators whose sole object is the preservation of God's truth rather than driving an agenda, God superintends in such fashion as to bring out a product that is reliable, truthful, perfect, infallible, and yes, still inspired!

As a matter of logic, it is notable that there is hypocrisy among those who insist that one must know the original languages of the Scripture (Hebrew, Aramaic and Greek) in order to fully comprehend God's word to man. Often these self-exalted teachers, preachers and authors will observe—and rightly so—that a particular Greek word found in the New Testament is translated into two or more different words in the English. These two or more words may be close in meaning or distant in meaning, but the "scholars" would have us to believe that, if a single Greek word is translated as one word in Scripture A and as another word in Scripture B, they have the authority to say it could have been—or should have been—translated in Scripture B as it was in Scripture A.

This argument breaks down when one applies simple logic. All languages contain words that have different meanings. Furthermore, all those differing meanings, whether they be nuances of the same meaning or unrelated meanings, have proper and improper usages. God certainly oversaw the translation of the King James Bible so as to prompt the translators to use the English word that conveyed the exact nuance. Of course he did! The use of a single Greek word translated several ways does not license someone today to presume that he can arbitrarily substitute one English word for the other in a "more readable" version.

Consider the English word mortal. This word can mean "deadly" as in the phrase "a mortal wound." The word can also mean "capable of dying; predisposed to eventual death" as in the concept of "a mortal being." Someone translating the word mortal out of English into some other language would have to select separate words in that second language to accurately represent the English author's intent, definition and connotation, or he would be guilty of twisting the meaning. So it is in the translation of the King James out of the trusted Hebrew Masoretic Text and the Greek Textus Receptus. The King James translation committee was guided by the overseeing Preserver of Scripture, the Holy Spirit, the Author of the original autographa who had (and still has) far more interest in preservation than any mere mortal!

Having eyes to see across the ages, the Spirit of God knew back in the 1500s that prior to the end of the church age a new language called English would be dominant in world communication. Possessing as He did (and does) such knowledge, the Holy Ghost stirred King James I of England to a task of authorizing a translation into English much as He stirred the King of Persia to authorize the rebuilding of the temple centuries earlier. With Holy Spirit oversight from Heaven and British monarchial authority upon earth, those scholars gave the world the King James Bible. It is a reliable, accurate, perfect English representation of God's exact thoughts and words, and he who understands English can understand God's message in the English King James Bible.

By the end of the first century, God had cited two of the seven churches addressed in Revelation with regard to "the deeds of the Nicolaitans" (Revelation 2:6) and "the doctrine of the Nicolaitans" (Revelation 2:15). The church at Ephesus was commended for hating the deeds, and the church at Pergamos was reprimanded for holding the doctrine of this group. What were the deeds and doctrine of the Nicolaitans? This group believed and practiced a conquest of the people via an exalted priesthood elevated over a subjugated congregation.

Simply stated, the word *nicolaitan* finds its roots in two Greek words: *nikao* meaning "to conquer" and *laos* meaning "the people." From those two words, a transliterated, assimilated compound word was formed. Transliteration from Greek to English is the process of transcribing Greek letter for corresponding English letter in the forming of the new word. Assimilation is the slight change in spelling for the sake of pronunciation ease. Thus *nikaolaos* became *nicolaitan*.

Because the word *nicolaitan* is not a translated word, this reference to the original language to explain a possibly unfamiliar word is not a contradiction of the chapter in which it appears. Transliterated words do require knowledge of the original letters and language. Translated words require no such knowledge because they are understood in the language into which they are translated.

Let it never be said that we who are inspirationist and preservationist fundamentalists are in any way guilty of severing preachers and teachers from their congregations by means of a literary nicolaitanism whereby only a trained few can really know what the Bible means.

9

English Words for an English-Speaking People

Having established in the previous chapter that God has truly authorized that English-speaking people have the Scripture in English, it naturally and logically follows that some space be given to English words themselves. The multiversion crowd has made much ado with regard not only to the specificity but also to the flexibility of the original languages of Scripture—Hebrew, Greek and even Aramaic—while at the same time these people lament the inability of the English language to convey meaning appropriately and accurately. Generally, proponents of this "crippled English" position are the people who are insisting that everyone in the English-speaking world who would really understand the Bible must become versed in those original Scripture languages.

It is the position of this writer, and of any person who has ever studied the English language with any intensity, that English is an amazingly well-adapted medium of communication. At issue is not the impossibility of conveying true meaning via translation from Hebrew or Greek into the English language. At issue in the "crippled English" argument are at least three separate factors: (1) that the Bible student of the late twentieth and early twenty-first centuries is more concerned with being "politically correct" than he is with being biblically and historically honest; (2) that the average reader of English today is only semieducated with regard to the definitions, connotations and usages of words in his own language, and (3) that the present-day degeneration of the English "slanguage" has resulted in disuse of several specific English words from our general vernacular.

Crippled English Due to Moral Degeneracy. Multiplied dozens of Bible passages that are reworded, rephrased or, even worse, removed from modern versions have been reworded, rephrased or removed based on the fact that the King James English is "aggressively pointed," as neo-evanglicals are often heard to say. "Aggressively pointed" at what? The compromising Christian avoids that question and proceeds to say that King James English does not "really apply" to today's problems and makes people in the pew feel "uncomfortable." What these nondenominational and interdenominational churchlings are actually admitting is that the King James English is so pithy and poignant that it really *does apply* to today's problems, and the fact that the King James English applies so succinctly is the reason people in the pews feel uncomfortable.

This denigrating attitude toward the venerable King James Version is appalling! Such individuals and movements as those calling for new versions of Scripture almost annually to keep pace with the changing and ever degenerating moral climate of what is called Christian society are catering to moral degeneration. Worse, by catering to that moral degeneration, they are further contributing to it. The crippling of English has come about because a society—indeed, a pseudo-Christian religious society—wants to increase its pew-sitters, even if it means doing so at the expense of overlooking the fact that many are brazenly living in moral sin. To do so, the inspired, preserved King James Bible must be replaced with a reworded, rephrased version that removes many of those words and passages that make immoral people feel uncomfortable. This tailoring of religion to fit one's lifestyle is a far cry from the tailoring of one's life by the Word of God as the Book of Acts shows.

The King James Version is so pointed about the moral issues of this millennium that the tolerance crowd wants to dilute the message so that there is no edge or point to the sword. One might ask a medieval knight for the use of an edgeless, pointless sword and get the reply that its only use would be for games. And is that Middle Ages warrior correct? Yes, he is. For that reason, the sport of fencing uses an épée, a sword that can do little or no harm. Indeed, a watered-down Scripture may be good for Bible games, but it will do no harm to the Devil or to the moral troubles of our day. An "épée" will give no victory in the spiritual battles in which true believers must engage "against principalities, against powers, against the rulers of the darkness of this world, against spiritual wickedness in high places" (Ephesians 6:12).

The matchless English of the King James Version, God's inspired, preserved revelation to the English-speaking world, uses words like *abomination, wicked, evil, unclean,* and *defiled,* words that run cross-grained upon the calloused, seared, defiled consciences of tolerant, open-minded souls who want acceptance of everything and denunciation of nothing. All too absent in the vernacular of our day is the clear-cut categorization of what is really happening. In the name of not judging, all honest judgment is discarded. Hence, the King James English which is profoundly applicable in a day of decadence in culture, the arts, etiquette, and education—that one say not Christianity itself—is deemed inappropriate or too pointed.

King James English includes words like *concupiscence, fornication, lasciviousness, sodomite,* and *adultery.* These words and others of similar nature denounce the modern-day debauchery of family and society. No town or city in the English-speaking world is untouched by the epidemic of infidelity to God in the matter of pure morals. Hardly a family, even in fundamental churches, is unscarred and unscathed by this plague of disregard for high and holy standards that protect the integrity of godly men and the loveliness of godly ladies. The truth is that such words are too applicable to the moral cesspool in which the English-speaking world is swimming, not that such words are not applicable enough! The moral decline of English-speaking peoples abhors such categorizations and prefers softer, less condemnatory terminology in order that sin not be exceeding sinful.

Again, the reader of the King James Bible encounters words like *obey, submit, subjection, master, servant,* etc. Do not these words cut like a sword through the rebellious humanism of the twenty-first century? Yes, they do; and for that reason alone, the new versions are changing the words, adding and subtracting for readability and relevance—so the translators and publishers say—to avoid the possibility of readers coming into contact with such "divisive" words. Again, is it not obvious that the problem is not that the King James Bible is not applicable enough, but that it is so applicable that its miracle status is proven? Of course! However, new versions use lighter and more comfortable words to accommodate the moral decline of both state and nation.

Spiritual decline, moral decline, civil decline—none of these can be denied. The twenty-first century is witness to the most godless paganism, the most atrocious immorality and the most lawless citizenry that has occupied this planet since Noah's Flood and Lot's Sodom and Gomorrah. No wonder Jesus said,

> "And as it was in the days of Noe, so shall it be also in the days of the Son of man.
> "They did eat, they drank, they married wives, they were given in marriage, until the day that Noe entered into the ark, and the flood came, and destroyed them all.
> "Likewise also as it was in the days of Lot; they did eat, they drank, they bought, they sold, they planted, they builded;
> "But the same day that Lot went out of Sodom it rained fire and brimstone from heaven, and destroyed them all.
> "Even thus shall it be in the day when the Son of man is revealed"—Luke 17:26–30.

This writer contends that the King James Version is absolutely applicable to the moral problems and blights that are plaguing modern society. It is categorically applicable, patently applicable, totally applicable! Its language is not unapplicable, but unapplied. Saying that the King James Bible is not applicable to today's societal ills is akin to saying that new paint is not applicable to a dilapidated building. The problem is that the perfect, sound language of that venerable Book has not been applied. The paint is still in the can.

Crippled English Due to Educational Deficiency. Due to a drastically deficient public education system in our nation, high school graduates and even those who have undergraduate degrees from college score low on world literacy scales. The eager student of Scripture, therefore, needs a grounded understanding of the actual words found in the Bible. Such understanding will include knowledge of definition, connotation and usage of the specific words found in God's inspired, preserved Scriptures.

As proof that this condition exists, ask the everyday, run-of-the-mill high school graduate, or better yet the average holder of a bachelor's degree from any public college or state university, to define *concupiscence, lasciviousness* or *wantonness*, words common to Scripture and to

98

the proper understanding of God's true character and untainted message to mankind. On the flip side, ask any American high school graduate or bachelor's degree recipient from today's education system to define *sanctification, consecration, justification,* or *propitiation.* Again, these beautiful words so incumbent upon the student of Scripture to know and use are completely divorced from the minds of our secularized, dumbed-down culture.

The fact is that educational deficiency is largely the product of political correctness, the progressive paralysis that is turning the English language (and just about everything else in society at large) into a wheelchair-bound quadriplegic. The comforts of the cowardly stance demand political correctness. The popularity of the sleazy morals of Hollywood mentality demands political correctness. The arrogance of the educational intellectualism of public education requires political correctness.

Crippled English Due to Conversational Disuse. "People just don't talk that way anymore!" the man exclaimed as this writer attempted to defend the superior language of the King James Scriptures against the inaccuracies of a modern translation. What is sad is that he inadvertently admitted his personal ignorance of even some very simple English words. Sadder still is that that man expressed the dangerous ignorance of his generation. But the thing that is saddest of all is that what he said is true. People do not talk like the Bible any more. Rather than elevate conversational expression to include the beautiful, the lovely, the accurate, and the truthful, the present generation seems content and intent upon corrupting conversational expression to the basest levels of what is ugly, dirty and trashy.

The obvious question one must ask is "Why?" Why has a whole catalogue of useful words on spiritual, moral, ethical, and cultural subjects been expunged from common vernacular and descried as *dinosaurish* and bygone? The obvious answer lies in the reality that such words are not "hip" or "awesome" or "cool." The spiritual apostasy, moral debauchery, ethical chicanery, and conversational misery of our day has thrown out the best for the average and then thrown out the average for the subnormal.

Clerics and laics alike who hold to the multiversion position of Scripture existence are often heard to call the King James Version *obso-*

lete, irrelevant or even *moldy*. Ascribing such words to the venerable King James Bible that was the backbone of both Great Awakenings and has been the text for every major revival in the history of the English-speaking world reveals that the conversational disuse of our time has led our society to invent new tools that don't work to replace an aged tool that worked very well.

God is taken down by common terminology that describes him as "cool" or "awesome" because that is the expressive limit of an uneducated and untrained society. While this may be the best way for an immature believer to express his views of God, this type of language should not be the norm for pulpits or the public ministry of the Word of God. Especially in the matter of this book, the inspiration-preservation issue, we must see that God is being belittled when modern translations are marketed for their relevance and that relevance is defined by an accommodation to rap lingo, "slanguage" and sloppy expression.

God deserves to be lifted up with our language. The Scripture terminology of God as high and lifted up is the way the Holy Spirit chose to inspire and preserve the very thoughts He has regarding Himself. The par for our pulpits ought to reflect the glory and majesty of our God, thus giving people that which is worthy of high aim and aspiration. While this is not a call for elitist language and stuffy expression, it is a call for lifting up the name and character of God with language that is true, honest, just, pure, lovely, of good report, virtuous, and praiseworthy (See Philippians 4:8).

To conclude this subject, it is safe to say that the King James Bible is the most applicable message in any field to the heart of the twenty-first-century globalist whose life is being lived, as those in Noah's day lived theirs, on the cusp of worldwide judgment at the end of one dispensation and near the beginning of another. The King James Bible is the most applicable message in the biblical arena to the heart of the twenty-first-century neo-evangelical whose life is being lived, as Lot lived, in the cesspool of the world with the stench of its rot all about him. The King James Bible is the most applicable message to the soul of the twenty-first-century independent, fundamental, Bible-believing separatist whose life is being lived, as Elijah lived, standing in the presence of God and proclaiming the message that all the modernist Ahabs and neo-evangelical Obadiahs loathe to hear.

Remember this. The King James Bible applies. Oh yes! With that in mind, the following subjects are pertinent to the study of Scriptures.

Word Definition. English is not a crippled language, but rather a language of much agility and ability in expressing precision. Many English words have diverse, unrelated meanings. The word *run* illustrates what must be seen along this vein. This word can be a verb with several meanings: (1) "to go faster than a walk" as in one's running a race; (2) "to move about without restraint" as in chickens running free in a farmyard; (3) "to make a quick, easy trip" as in running to the store; (4) "to enter an election race" as in running for office; (5) "to unravel lengthwise" as in hosiery running; (6) "to sing or play scales" as in one's fingers running up the keyboard; (7) "to go back and forth in a prescribed route" as in a train running between Washington, D.C., and Baltimore; (8) "to continue in force of operation" as in a business running well; (9) "to flow" as in blood running from an open wound; (10) "to direct" as in running a factory; and more! As a noun, the word *run* can have the corresponding noun function definitions that go with many of the already stated verb meanings. On top of those, the word run in its noun form may mean (1) "a point made in baseball" as in scoring a run; (2) "the direction in which a vein of ore lies" as in a run of iron; (3) "that which flows within a certain time lapse" as in the first run of sap from a maple tree; (4) a quantity of work turned out" as in a run of ten thousand copies of a magazine; (5) "the usual or normal kind or character" as in the average run of workers or the run of the mill; (6) "freedom of movement or access" as in having the run of the shop; (7) "an enclosure frequented by or restricted for animals" as in a dog's run; (8) "an inclined course" as in a bobsled run; (9) "an unbroken course of performances" as in a two-week run for a high school play; (10) "a painting defect caused by excessive flow" as in a run down the side of the building; and more.

All this detail about the word *run* is written so that the student of Scripture may see that English words are versatile, flexible tools, not "crippled" and irrelevant in their expression. While the word *run* is extraordinary in its multiple uses, and while the average English word is restricted to fewer definitions, the truth is that English is a language well capable of varied and exact expression. The need is not to rewrite, reword and replace the Bible. The need is to read what is written and learn what is meant by what is written.

This applies to words common in the King James Bible such as *wine*, which may mean "the fresh juice of newly pressed grapes," "the lees of freshly trodden grapes," or "alcoholic beverage that produces drunkenness." Context and common sense will always tell the reader which one is meant. No violation is done to God or his character when the reader adjusts himself to the proper definition of the word. All the Scripture reads without contradiction when the obvious definition of the word *wine* is understood.

Another example of this is the Bible's usage of the phrase *principalities and powers*. When this phrase is used in Ephesians 3:10, the obvious meaning is the hierarchy of heavenly angels who are "ministering spirits, sent forth to minister for them who shall be heirs of salvation" (Hebrews 1:14). In Colossians 2:15, however, this identical phrase is clearly a reference to Satan and his demonic hierarchy of unclean "angels which kept not their first estate, but left their own habitation" (Jude 1:6). Ephesians 6:12 also refers to this definition of the phrase when it addresses the believer's wrestling not with flesh and blood but with principalities and powers and rulers of darkness and spiritual wickedness. Finally, a third definition of this phrase is employed in Titus 3:1 where context clearly makes plain that the principalities and powers are earthly authorities ordained of God to maintain civil law and order.

A study far too detailed and involved for the space in this book would be a thorough investigation into all the definitions of the word *for* as they appear in the Scripture. If one definition is applied to all, many passages would be confusing at best and senseless at worst. This little word can be a preposition, a coordinating conjunction, or a subordinating conjunction; furthermore, in each of these three separate word functions, multiple definitions are possible. Think of I Peter 4:6 which begins, "For for this cause..." That verse would pose difficulty if one failed to study different meanings and functions of the word *for*, two of which are found here in back-to-back succession.

Word Connotation. A word's definition is its exact meaning or meanings, while the connotation of a word is its usage or understood meaning. For example, the words *famous* and *infamous* both mean "well known"; however, the connotation of *famous* is "well known in a good way and for honorable reason," while the connotation of *infamous* is "well known in a bad way and for a dishonorable reason." Both David and Ahab are well-known kings of Israel; however, David was famous, but Ahab was infamous.

Connotation of King James Bible words is important as well. An interesting study on this line involves the word *catch* which means "to seize, snatch or lay hold." The connotation of this word in Luke 5:10 is favorable. Jesus Christ told Peter after the catching of the miraculous draught of fish, "Fear not; from henceforth thou shalt catch men." Peter, always a fisherman, would simply employ the same methods he had previously used to seize fish so he could sell them and make a living to seize men from the clutches of Hell to deliver them to learn how to live. It was a good catching, a positive thing. The Lord was telling Peter that the future held a productive and fulfilling activity for him: catching men.

However, Luke uses the word *catch* a few chapters later in a most unfavorable connotation. Here its connotation is seizure for evil purpose, not for good purpose. When the Lord was denouncing woe upon the Pharisees and lawyers, they "began to urge him vehemently, and to provoke him to speak of many things: Laying wait for him, and seeking to catch something out of his mouth, that they might accuse him" (11:53, 54). These rabid hypocrites sought to snatch a word or phrase from his lips and tear it from its contextual moorings and use it against him.

Whether it is the word *catch* or any other of hundreds of Bible words that possess multiple connotations, one must know which connotation is intended in order to comprehend fully the passage where the word is used.

Word Usage. Because words can be fickle and unpredictable, an avid student of Scripture must explore all the usages of a word to see the intent of the Holy Spirit. In navigating the waters of word usage, it is important to note that, upon rare occasions, some English words have entirely opposite usages! The word *cleave* can be used in a context to

103

convey the idea of splitting apart as in Ecclesiastes 10:9, while it is used in a different verse to illustrate a holding together as found in Genesis 2:24. What about the word *let*, which is usually used to communicate allowance or permission, but in rare usages, such as in Isaiah 43:13 and II Thessalonians 2:7, the word is used to communicate prohibition or prevention?

Dictionary. With all this information as background, the writer advises that every Christian should purchase and use a good English dictionary. Because of its renderings of the honest meanings that were widely accepted prior to the degeneracy of formal and conversational English, *The American Dictionary of the English Language,* 1828 Edition, is available from many publishers. This reprint of Noah Webster's masterpiece gives the student of the English Bible all the definitive and connotative help that is needed for the study of English words used in the King James Bible. In fact, many of the examples given to illustrate definitions are Scripture quotations. This characteristic alone sets this dictionary apart from the updated and modern dictionaries which have omitted many biblical definitions and usages. Most dictionaries published since 1950 are modernized to accommodate the moral degeneration, educational deficiency and conversational disuse cited earlier in this chapter.

Concordance. Another book that is vital to understanding of the King James Bible is *Strong's Exhaustive Concordance of the Bible.* This massive volume may intimidate at first sight, but its beautiful layout, its comprehensive listing of every word in every usage in the Bible, its Hebrew and Greek dictionaries, its numbering system, and all its other offerings make it more than valuable to the student of Scripture.

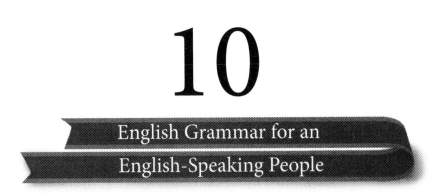

10

English Grammar for an
English-Speaking People

Grammar, the unmentionable abomination in all Bible study, is laughed at, loathed and lamented, but seldom loved. However, when God authorized the writing of Scripture, he superintended the writers' use of the various tools of verbal communication: language and syntax, verbs and nouns, capital letters and question marks, etc. Simply put, grammar includes the study of the relationships between words that results in sensible sentences and comprehensible expression.

Any person who yearns to understand Scripture in his own language must possess a basic knowledge of the grammar of that language. He must recognize that nouns name; that verbs act or link; that adjectives modify nouns or pronouns; that adverbs can describe verbs, adjectives or other adverbs; that pronouns replace nouns; that conjunctions join; that prepositions relate; and that interjections exclaim.

Furthermore, he will need an understanding of some basic grammatical functions. A noun or pronoun can function as a subject, predicate noun, direct object, indirect object, object of a preposition, objective complement, or appositive. Verbs may function as action (transitive or intransitive) or state of being words; as active or passive in voice; as indicative, imperative or subjunctive in mood; as present, past, future, or perfect in tense; as progressive or punctual in time; or as verbals whose function is description and naming.

Moreover, the student who wants to understand the Bible in his own tongue must have a working knowledge of punctuation. Some punctuation rules have been either modified over the centuries of English usage or introduced as the language has developed. For instance, modern English punctuation employs quotation marks around the exact words of a speaker, but the King James English Bible has no quotation marks. Other punctuation rules and marks have remained relatively static in usage for the duration of time that English has been a language. The King James Bible is simple in that its primary punctuation distinctions are commas, periods, semicolons, colons, question marks, exclamation points, and capital letters. These seven uncomplicated marks have nearly the identical usage today that they had at the very inception of English as a language. They serve in every context of the King James Bible to illuminate the reader as to the intention of the Author in His original giving of the Word of God.

Generally understood, capital letters begin new sentences, proper names and direct quotations. Commas not only set off introductory elements at the beginning of a sentence but also separate related words or phrases in a series. Semicolons and colons serve as separators of longer phrases or clauses. Periods end complete declarative and imperative sentences. Question marks finalize questions, and exclamation points are used when the sentence communicates strong emotion or dire command. While this is an oversimplification of King James Bible punctuation, it is relatively accurate and will help to give clarity to original, intended meaning.

Finally, Bible students who want to know the Bible should have adequate knowledge of letter usage and the spelling of words. Changes in the shapes of letters themselves, such as the alteration from the archaic f-shaped *s* to the present-day curved letter were part of that young language coming into usage. Spelling differences of the same word also developed, as in the insertion of a *j* in place of the *i* and the replacement of the old *ie* ending with a *y* ending so that the "olde" word *maiestie* became the modern word *majesty*. Other spelling changes involved the dropping of a final *e* or a doubled consonant or both in some words as the language matured so that *farre* became *far*. None of these changes involved removing words, adding words or changing words for other words. Instead, these alterations were literal without changing the exact word.

The several translations of the 1500s were not the perfecting of an imperfect Word of God. Rather, they were necessary steps in placing the Scripture into the language of the English-speaking world when the English language was in its infancy and developing as a tongue of use in the world. The difference between the development of the language in the sixteenth and seventeenth centuries and the multiversion approach of the twentieth and twenty-first centuries is that the ancient translations were an accommodation to a language that was arriving at its expressive perfection while the present-day paraphrases and translations are an accommodation to the decaying of the English language to its expressive perversion. Again, the discrepancies found in ancient English translations are accommodations that cooperate with the changes within a language, not aberrations that allow for the changes within a culture!

Every word ever uttered by the Holy Ghost and recorded by "holy men of God" who were "moved" by Him was uttered and recorded within a grammatical relationship with other words in the same sentence. Every sentence ever spoken by God and placed on paper was spoken and then placed on paper by one of those holy men in a grammatical relationship with other sentences. Every passage of God's holy Word ever inspired by God and penned by a holy man of God was inspired and penned in a grammatical context with other passages. Every book of Scripture that the Holy Ghost authored and that godly men wrote was authored and written in a grammatical context with all the other books of Scripture.

Faith does not serve grammatical context, but grammatical context serves any faith effort in understanding what God said and meant. All true study of God's Word runs amok whenever the reader seeks to dissociate the content from the grammar of the content. While audiences or individuals may groan over the explanation of the grammar of a passage that shows that a participle is describing a noun and is not the actual verb of the sentence, or that the truth of a verse ending with a comma is obviously continued in the next verse, such explanation is important. These trivialities are the stuff of communication, and the Scripture is God's communication to us! Content must always be connected to context.

Without some basic grammar skills, the average reader's attempt at gaining proper content from the context is a pin-the-tail-on-the-donkey exercise that seldom really finds the right position! However, a Spirit-filled deference to the grammar of any passage will yield the single intended meaning of the author (God himself) as opposed to the multiple meanings that can be derived when grammar and its associated aspects are ignored.

Present day public education systems that graduate one-third of all students across the board as functionally illiterate do not prepare many of our nation's children to read anything, to say nothing of the Scripture! Students who are graduating or have already graduated from high school or even from undergraduate levels of college may find themselves in a quagmire when grappling with even the simple concepts of English grammar.

All this considered, learning to love the English language and all its beauty so that the Scripture can speak the mind of God to the minds of men is of utmost importance. Such a love will be greatly enhanced if, in addition to the dictionary and concordance recommended in the previous chapter, each student of the Word of God purchases a grammar handbook, a Bible handbook and a Bible encyclopedia. Such volumes will be wonderful tools to help simplify the maze commonly called English grammar.

Grammar Handbook. One such product is the *Grammar Handbook* published by Landmark Freedom Baptist Curriculum. With a Holy-Spirit-motivated zeal, one or two years of reference to such a handbook, and perhaps a bit of coaching, most teenagers and adults can develop a good command of the basic grammar of the English language.

Bible Handbook. Beyond the grammar handbook, this writer recommends a good Bible handbook, that addresses from a staunchly biblical and Baptist perspective some of the sticky wickets of the Bible. Many of the biblical difficulties are passages or wordings where the grammar or syntax is not easily discerned, even for a well-trained grammarian. A simple reminder is in order here. That reminder is that difficult passages in the English Bible are translated out of difficult passages in the Hebrew or Greek; therefore, being a student of Hebrew or Greek will not remove the difficulty. The answer to such difficulties is not the position that says English is incompetent to express another language.

The answer is to dig within one's own language to find proper meaning.

Bible Encyclopedia. This is a more extensive work than a Bible handbook. It will cover literally thousands of Bible topics. You should find one written from a biblical and Baptist perspective that is well researched, properly documented and accurately worded. Basic Scripture-related topics should be handled in their historic Baptist perspective with ample referencing to the Bible itself, leaving the student better informed. While this is not a grammar handbook, it will often refer to grammatical or syntactical details which will help in the comprehension of the King James Bible.

Of course, these books are not all the books a preacher or layperson should own. Good books are treasures, and students of Scripture may own as many as they please for their edification and understanding. These, however, are vital in navigating the waters of English grammar.

11

The New International Shakespeare
and the New American Standard Chaucer

Multiversion mentality is built, in part, upon the foolish supposition that no one can understand King James English! Other chapters of this book have been devoted to English words and the English language, but this additional material on the subject will not be overly redundant. Interestingly, this writer has read the King James Scriptures in its entirety nearly sixty times in the thirty-five-plus years of his Christian life. From the standpoint of literary readability, the King James Bible is more easily comprehensible than several of the modern versions, and certainly more readily understandable than Shakespeare or Chaucer. Where, then, is the *New International Shakespeare?* the *New American Standard Chaucer?* the *Good News for Modern Literary Studies?*

Professors of classical English literature would be quite miffed if they were asked to teach the classics in dumbed-down, modernized English. Indeed, much of the poetic and literary genius of those English writers (and of many non-English writers whose classic works have been translated into English) would vanish if their writings were updated to modern English expression. If meaning is *lost* by updating and modernizing of language in literature, how then can meaning be *gained* by updating and modernizing of language in Scripture?

Paradoxically, those who understand the archaic idiom and obsolete usages and spellings so frequently found in the classics of English literature and literature based in other languages are considered well rounded and educated and erudite, while those who would promote the same level of understanding of the few archaic or obsolete words found in the King James text are called precisionists, obscurantists and other less desirable terms. Why is it so admirable for students of literary classics to develop at least a working knowledge of the old words, but it is deemed ludicrous and unnecessary—or even impossible—for students of the English Bible to use and understand old words? One wonders...

Since this is a chapter making comparisons, one might be interested to note that Shakespeare used nearly twenty thousand different words in his writings, while the King James Bible uses only about six thousand separate words. Eighty-two percent of the words in the Sermon on the Mount and 250 of the 319 words in the Ten Commandments are of one syllable. The issue is not the readability or the understandability of the Bible. God made sure his time-honored, now-four-centuries-old King James Bible for the English world was far simpler than classical English literature. If anything is to be revised, let it be Shakespeare and Chaucer, but leave the Scripture as is.

The following poetic piece shows the value of the Scripture as it towers dauntingly above all the works of men. Bringing its wording down to the level of cultural acceptance or educational averageness would tarnish its glory, diminish its beauty, and establish its debility.

> This precious Book I'd rather own
>   Than all the golden gems
> That e'er in monarch's coffers shone,
>   Than all their diadems.
> Nay, were the sea one chrysolite,
>   The earth a golden ball,
> And diamonds all the stars of night,
>   This Book were worth them all.
>
> —William Leggett

Dumbing down of any subject does not enhance the learning of any student. Yes, students should enroll at their academic levels and move upward, but let us remember that the Bible is not merely—or primarily—an academic book. Scripture addresses many academic subjects: history, astronomy, geology, physics, chemistry, biology, genetics, arithmetic and mathematics, and a host of others. However, the Word of God is first and foremost a book of eternal truth from the tongue and breath of God; and by virtue of its all-encompassing nature, it happens also to contain accurate historical, scientific and mathematical information.

Forgotten, or at least ignored, in this generation of "making the Scripture easy to read" is the entire concept of divine teaching. The indwelling Holy Spirit is called the Spirit of truth (John 14:17; 15:26; 16:13), and it is He who is promised by the Father to guide the reader of Scripture into all truth. Why then is there all this hullabaloo about reducing the Scripture to a level of understandability? Why is there not a focus upon the believer falling upon his face before God in humble dependence in order that God's Spirit may indeed perform his teaching capacity in the reader's spirit? The answer lies not in the need for ignorant people to have simplicity, but in the need for arrogant people to have humility! Scripture does not need to be rewritten at the expense of its purity and holiness. Instead, people need to be regenerated and renewed in the spirit of their minds and revived in heart and soul in order that they may receive spiritual truths.

Furthermore, one must consider the other side of learning: teaching. While the study of Scripture strictly from an academic basis omits the reliance upon the Holy Spirit's enlightenment, the teaching of Scripture exclusively from a scholarly basis also omits the place of the Holy Spirit. No seminary professor or Bible department dean has any right or calling to usurp the superior place of the Holy Spirit in the impartation of divine truth to his students. Whenever a Bible college professor fails or refuses to admit that his own teaching ability and content are secondary, he has crossed a line that is intolerable in the eyes of God. Needed in every Bible college, Christian university and seminary in our land is a revival of truly spiritual teaching methods. Professors are merely mouthpieces who ought to take careful heed to James 3:1 just as solemnly as they expect their pulpit-pounding counterparts to do! No man has popish authority to "interpret" and finagle and manipulate Scripture.

Several thoughts, therefore, are significant in one's efforts to gain spiritual knowledge from the mine of God's Word. Whether from the teaching side or from the learning side—or both—these guidelines will serve well to accomplish two things as individuals seek to grow in their knowledge of God and his truth. First, the following parameters will entirely eliminate the need for new versions on the basis of readability or ease of understanding. Second, each of the ensuing concepts will elevate the place of the Holy Spirit and subjugate the place of man in the process of learning the Bible.

No Private Interpretation. In all Scripture study, Scripture must govern and give credibility to the intended and permanent meaning of all related Scripture because "no prophecy of the scripture is of any private interpretation" (II Peter 1:20). Peter's usage of the word *interpretation* is not in the sense of interpreting from one language to another as is the case in Mark 15:22 where the Hebrew word *Golgotha* is interpreted, that is, translated, "The place of a skull." Neither did Peter employ the word *interpretation* in the way the Old Testament refers to giving the allegorical analogy of a dream. Rather, the apostle Peter was directed by the Holy Ghost to use this word to mean "explanation."

Furthermore, Peter described interpretation with the specific adjective *private*. This word means "pertaining to self or one's own; separate; isolated." What is obvious therefore from this statement is that no one Scripture verse or portion has an explanation that is exclusive to itself, but every Scripture verse or portion has an explanation that is inclusive of what all other Scripture verses or portions say about the same subject.

Such cohesiveness as is found in the eternal Word of God is possible only due to what Peter says next in his Epistle, that "holy men of God spake as they were moved by the Holy Ghost" (II Peter 1:21). God directed each human writer to give specific truth about various subjects such that all the truth about those various subjects found within the pages of Scripture forms one glorious cord of interpretive unity. When one pores over the glorious parts of the Bible with this mind-set, he needs no dumbing down or changing of words, because one verse clears up another, and one passage explains another to the peaceful satisfaction of the spiritual reader.

Proper Interpretation. Continuous debate from denominational positions, theological persuasions and personal experience with regard to what this or that Bible verse "really means" often crosses the line into mysticism. With smugness and assurance, the arguers resign to the cop-out statement, "That's your interpretation." Unaware of their own ignorance, those who parrot such a sentence are actually admitting that they believe the plain truths of Scripture are actually interpretable in as many ways as there are interpreters!

As has already been indicated, interpretation has more than one meaning. In Scripture, dreams, parables, names, and tongues are to be interpreted. The interpretation of dreams allowed for hidden meanings to be revealed. When Daniel interpreted Nebuchadnezzar's "statue dream," the hidden meanings of the four metals on the statue were made known. Interpretation of parables provided for questionable applications to be explained. When the apostles asked Jesus the meaning of certain parables, He interpreted those parables, giving the Spirit-inspired representations as was the case when he told the apostles, "The seed is the word of God" (Luke 8:11). Names in Scripture were interpreted in meaning so that Bible readers might understand that Cephas, Jesus' particular name for Simon Peter, meant "a stone."

The interpretation of languages in Scripture, a broad and often-confused subject in this day of religious apostasy, was and is simply a process of translating so that an individual speaking one language could understand someone speaking a different language. This meaning of interpretation is found in the Acts' account of the Day of Pentecost and in the Corinthian account of guidelines for speaking in tongues within the New Testament church.

However, there is no place where God suggests or in any manner indicates that His laws, commandments, precepts, judgments, or testimonies are to be interpreted in the sense meant when someone says, "That's your interpretation." To interpret God's laws, commandments, precepts, judgments, or testimonies in that sense diminishes His Word to the level of the "private interpretation" which Peter categorically denied. How, then, does the Holy Spirit help the spiritual believer to understand God's law, command, precept, judgment, or testimony? What is the role of the Spirit, and what is the role of the reader in finding the meaning of God's law or command or precept or judgment, or testimony? Simply stated, the role of the Holy Ghost is revelation, that is, inspiration of a human writer to record the specific, unchangeable, exact words of the particular law, command, precept, judgment, or testimony in question. Then, the role of the spiritual reader is to accept that law, command, precept, judgment, or testimony by faith. When the spiritual reader accepts God's revelation by faith and refuses to enter into his own "private interpretation," he can understand.

Therefore, if one of God's laws is to be understood, it must be heeded. A law is an authoritative statement of God wherein he makes known His unalterable, sovereign dealings with His created world. Vance Havner, the revivalist of the 1940s through the 1980s, said, "You might as well attack Gibraltar with a popgun as to attack the moral law of the universe and the God who rules in righteousness." What Brother Havner was admitting is that God's laws, no matter how they are attacked or beseiged, will never be damaged in the least. They stand. They remain.

For example, the law of male and female established in Creation and taught throughout the Word of God will never be understood by left-wingers who want to deny it; furthermore, middle-of-the-roaders who want to trim that law's edges to make allowances and compromises will never understand either. However, that beautiful law of God's constant dealing with His created beings and things is understood by even the least educated among his saints who simply accept that law by faith and live within its parameters. This writer knows of some Ph.D.s who are involved in billion-dollar research projects into the issue of male and female as this culture attempts to blur those lines and make allowances for those who want to blot out those lines. However, this writer also knows some farm boys who have not yet graduated from high school who understand that if a farmer wants his herd to multiply, he needs a bull to mingle with the cows!

What about understanding God's commandments, those authoritative statements of God telling man to do or not do a certain thing? The commandments of God often include the words "thou shalt" or the words "thou shalt not." Should someone want to understand one of God's commandments, he need not consult a dozen commentators—some or all of whom might offer variant "interpretations." Rather, all he need do is obey that commandment. Then he will understand it. No command is ever fully understood until is it obeyed.

When Paul commanded the New Testament believer to give thanks in everything (I Thessalonians 5:18), he prompted a firestorm of objections. One person asks, "How can I thank God for troubles?" Another just as incredulously asks, "How can I be grateful for pain?" Still another poses the question, "How can I count it all joy when I endure trials?" These and dozens more questions can make that command impossible to understand. But know this one thing—the quiet, Spirit-filled believer who may or may not have a college degree or even a high school diploma but who just thanks God for everything understands that command. Understanding God's commandments is reserved to those who obey them, not to those who "interpret them."

The same can be said of God's judgments, that is, his statements of what is right and what is wrong. Lying is defined as wrong, and telling the truth is defined as right because God judged it so. No other reason! God decided this, and it is written in the heart of man to be thus. But listen to the objections of those who want to "interpret" all the different times when it seems so right to do what God has judged as wrong. These interpreters of God's judgment want to propose that lying is permissible in instances where the truth might hurt someone's feelings, in cases where truth might be unpopular, in circumstances where the truth might cost something, or in situations where the truth might not have a humanly favorable or humanly visible outcome. Such people will never understand God's judgments, no matter how long and diligently they study them. But let a person simply appropriate the judgments of God, and by faith he will understand far more than the educated compromiser will ever comprehend.

More could be said with regard to the faith-acceptance of clearly revealed truth in God's forever Word. All in all, those who appropriate God's precepts know more of God's truth than those who attempt to "interpret" black ink on white paper. God intended his Word to be read, heard, believed, acknowledged, and practiced—no arguments, no confusions, no compromises, no disclaimers, no interpretations; just acceptance, compliance and obedience.

Let it be clearly stated that the faith that heeds God's law will understand far more than the scholarship that hedges on that law in the name of enlightenment. The faith that obeys God's commandments will perceive far more than the scholarship that obfuscates those same commandments for the sake of political correctness. The faith that appropriates God's judgments will discern far more of God's truth than the scholarship that adjusts God's judgments to the ideas and customs of the present culture. And it is just this faith that logically leads to the next topic.

Faith Above Findings. All diligent effort to uncover and discover the nuggets of truth in God's Word must elevate faith above findings. Hebrews 11:3 boldly declares that understanding is through faith. Doubtless, the study of God's eternal book is a faith venture! This venture must be entered in full trust that the Holy Ghost who is the Author will enlighten the reader.

Whenever the pursuit of Scripture understanding utilizes a teaching or learning process that ascribes more credibility to one's findings than to faith in the Author Himself, that teaching or learning process is doomed to eventual and ultimate—if not immediate—failure.

Paul's declaration "through faith we understand" (Hebrews 11:3) encompasses much more than a singular statement about creation. Paul referred also to the fact that what one cannot see, one can understand and accept by faith. Many of the so-called Scriptural enigmas can be far better understood by faith than by findings. The full acceptance of both truths in their Scripture contexts yields understanding.

The Prince of Preachers, Charles Haddon Spurgeon (1834–1892), said, "I hold one single sentence out of God's Word to be of more certainty and of more power than all the discoveries of all the learned men of all the ages." That grand pastor of London's Metropolitan Tabernacle whose voice now offers sinless praises to God as it mingles with the songs of other saints awaiting resurrection had the right idea. He understood the infinite magnitude of faith in stark contrast to the strict limitation upon findings. He could see by the Spirit's enlightenment that believing God as he read one Bible passage gave him greater and more valuable help than he could reap from a lifetime in a laboratory.

Historical Context. The miraculous "all-profitableness" of Holy-Ghost-inspired truth involves a historical context, but that historical context will always enhance the truth that the Holy Spirit is teaching and never eliminate that deeper meaning. Modernists and liberals, neo-orthodoxists and neo-evangelicals, and even some fundamentalists will try to smooth over the rough edges of a hard-pill-to-swallow concept of Scripture with the wave of the hand and the comment: "Jesus meant something different in His historical context than what we understand in our day." Aside from bordering upon blasphemy, such a careless slur strongly indicates that the speaker does not believe that Scripture is profitable beyond the historical time period in which it was originally uttered!

Perhaps the most common subject to be relegated to the historical trash heap is the subject of Hell. Nonliteralists love to say that the Saviour's comments in the Gospels were a reference to the garbage dump outside Jerusalem where the fires burned and the maggots gnawed. Such a position exalts a historical fact above its obvious spiritual connection. No exegetical hat trick, however clever, can do away with the fact that our Saviour foresaw the eternal state of the unsaved as endless horror beyond a great gulf forever fixed. Historical context does not diminish what Jesus said. Historical context explains it, enhances it and enlarges it. Faith accepts the truth as illustrated by the historical realities of the day and age in which the truth was first spoken, but faith never allows those historical realities to hinder or limit the truth.

Rather than revise the Bible, the twenty-first-century believer should revisit it. With faith, proper interpretation and due respect to historical data, the beautiful King James Bible becomes a gold mine of understanding and wisdom. One need not have a dozen versions of the text on his shelf so he can consult them all and "discover" a meaning. Rather, he needs but the King James Bible if he is a speaker of English. That marvel of inspiration and preservation, standing now for four glorious centuries, is in no more need of revision to ensure modern understanding than the Matterhorn is in need of resculpting to maintain its grandeur!

12

Truth: Absolute or Approximate?

Truth is a concept with one absolute definition. However, understanding of any particular absolute truth may be affected by external factors. Ascribing the wrong connotation to the word as it is used in any given context will alter the entire understanding of that particular context.

Temporary Truth

A person standing outside on a summer day may truthfully and honestly report that the temperature is eighty-eight degrees on the Fahrenheit scale. However, by evening, what was truthful at three in the afternoon might no longer be true. With the cooling of the waning sun, perhaps that truthful and honest report of the temperature would be only eighty-one degrees. This is an example of truth that is temporary.

Other examples of temporary truth might be a person's stating that he is wearing a navy blue, pin-striped suit. That declaration might be true for eight or ten hours, but once he takes that suit off to change into his pajamas for the evening, that truth no longer exists.

Some temporary truth may last longer than other temporary truth. Perhaps a truth might last for three months, such as a statement that there is snow on the ground. A temporary truth might last for years, such as the idea that this or that person has brown hair. That temporary truth may change over time if the person's hair turns gray or white, or if the person goes bald and no longer has hair.

121

Approximate Truth

Approximate truth may cover the same realm as temporary truth. The individual cited above might say that the temperature was in the upper eighties and be honest and truthful without being absolute in his truthful statement. He might say he was wearing a dark blue suit, approximating the color without giving the specific color as navy blue. Dark blue might be a dark shade of royal blue, a dark shade of periwinkle blue or of some other specific shade including navy. Approximate truth is still true, but it is not specific.

Some approximate truth is more specific than other approximate truth. For instance, if Monday's weather forecast calls for rain, that approximates the fact that rain will fall during the day on Monday. A more specific forecast might detail the severity or amount of rainfall; the exact type of storm, whether shower or thunderstorm; the time of day of the precipitation, whether forenoon or afternoon or evening, etc. All levels of this approximate truth would be acceptable in weather forecasting; however, the more detailed the report is, the more helpful it would be to someone planning a picnic!

Eternally True

Any approach to the concept of Scripture inspiration and preservation that automatically presumes the "temporary truth mentality" or the "approximate truth mentality" will be flawed from its inception. While the Bible certainly records historic truths that are no longer reality, those temporary historic truths are absolutely true. Even though some records found in the Bible give approximations rather than detailed accounts, those approximations are absolutely irrefutable. The student of Scripture must approach the discipline of knowing God and the Word of God from the standpoint of the perfect accuracy of all truth corporately and every truth individually.

Consider one of the verses that Christians often use as an assurance verse: I John 5:13. This dynamic declaration appears in a portion wherein God the Author of eternal truth spells out his own opinion of "the record." Even a casual examination of I John 5:9–21 reveals some striking information. First, note that in verse nine, God relegates the accuracy and reliability of His record or witness as greater than any

122

record or witness of men. Second, observe verse ten where the Lord bluntly avers that any person who would deny the witness or record of God is calling God a liar. In the next two verses, God outlines with undeniable clarity what the witness or record is. It is upon this marvelous foundation that the grand verse of assurance, I John 5:13, is based. Forward from I John 5:13, God continues His defense of His witness or record as it relates to prayer and petitioning the throne room of Heaven, prayer and interceding for others in matters of sin, and prayer relative to knowing God in a world that lies in wickedness and crawls with idolatry.

Why would the Holy Ghost go to the length to which He went to contrast His witness to the witness of men if they were equivalent? If the temporary and approximate witness of men were of similar extent or synonymous value with the witness of God, verse nine would be a moot point. The witness or record of God, however, is not of the same quality as the witness of men! The witness and record of God are as high above the testimony of men as the sky is above the ground!

Why would the Lord devote such detailed defense of the witness or record that He had previously given of His Son in the writings of the prophets and apostles if those writings were only temporary or approximate truth? Since this particular portion about God's witness and record is found in the inspired and preserved writings of the apostle John written near the end of the first century, why not consider the record that God gave of His Son from just the other writings of John?

Are moderns to assume that the words between Jesus and Nicodemus are approximations of that conversation and that Jesus might have said, "Ye may be born again" or "Ye should be born again"? Are we twenty-first century believers to assume that Jesus "rounded up" when He spoke to the woman at the well and that she had actually had only four husbands? Should the "enlightened" Christian accept that the paralytic in John chapter five had honestly lain at the Pool of Bethesda for thirty-eight years, or would we be better served to accept that this was a random number selected to emphasize the man's desperation and he might have lain there for only twenty-nine years or perhaps he had lain there for forty-six years? Where does it all end?

How accurate is the story of the feeding of the five thousand? Were

123

there five loaves and two fishes or not? Was the lad little, or is he portrayed as little to sentimentalize the account and to tantalize the readers? Were twelve baskets full of fragments gathered, or were the fragments really gathered in hats or crates? Did Jesus really address only twelve at the end of this story, or did the Lord use this number to create a martyrdom scenario?

How accurate is the story in John chapter eight? Was the woman truly caught in adultery, or is this an accommodation to keep Bible readers on the edges of their seats? And what of the story in the ninth chapter about the man born blind? Was he perhaps blinded by an adolescent carelessness, but since the Lord needed a more miraculous sounding account, did He record that the man was born blind? At this point, this writer cries out: Stop it already. Enough of this meddling with the text!

Any thinking person is by this time aware of the ultimate result of relegating absolute truth to approximation and eternal truth to temporariness! In short order, and certainly in far fewer than twenty centuries, the truth would not be truth at all; and no reliability could ever be asserted with regard to any biblical witness or record!

Absolute Truth and Quotations. Perhaps this aspect of the absolute accuracy of Scripture is the one that most merits some honest questioning. When the Word of God says, "As it is written..." or "that it might be fulfilled..." and the fulfillment records slightly different words than the prophecy, is accuracy of the truth forfeited? When one considers quotations from the Old Testament as they are rendered in the New Testament, he is forced to approach them as either accurate or inaccurate. At the outset, let it be stated that seeming inaccuracies are just that: seeming inaccuracies. The Bible is totally and absolutely accurate, and every truth is an absolute truth.

Quotations of Partial Statements. One such seeming discrepancy regards what was actually written over the head of Jesus Christ as he hung upon the cross. Was it "THIS IS JESUS THE KING OF THE JEWS (Matthew 27:37), "THE KING OF THE JEWS" (Mark 15:26), "THIS IS THE KING OF THE JEWS" (Luke 23:38), or "JESUS OF NAZARETH THE KING OF THE JEWS" (John 19:19)? What did that title, authorized and perhaps actually written by the hand of Pontius Pilate, actually say?

Truth: Absolute or Approximate?

Simple comparison shows that all four Gospel writers used the name "King of the Jews." Each of the Gospel writers included whatever additional information the Holy Ghost inspired, and it is their wordings taken together that render the complete statement. The full message of the accusation written over Christ's head on that day was "This is Jesus of Nazareth the King of the Jews." This is not contradictory but complementary. This is not arbitrary but accurate.

Such combinations of testimony have been used since time immemorial, and all such combinations of accounting render the complete story. The details of one righteous witness corroborate the details of other righteous witnesses to produce absolute accuracy in the record of what was actually written, spoken or done in any given situation. For this reason, the Lord wrote such a provision into the ancient law of Israel when He said, "At the mouth of two witnesses, or at the mouth of three witnesses, shall the matter be established" (Deuteronomy 19:15). Furthermore, this method was included in Christ's teachings on church discipline (Matthew 18:16); in Paul's entreaty with regard to the Corinthians' repentance (II Corinthians 13:1); and in Paul's instruction to Timothy concerning confrontation of pastors (I Timothy 5:19). Certainly if such a method were reliable in noninspired settings for the words of men, it would be all the more reliable in the Holy Spirit's giving of the sacred record of God's Word.

Quotations of Spoken Statements. A vast difference may exist between what certain prophets spoke in their public ministries and what the Holy Ghost had them write down as inspired Scripture. In Matthew 27:9, 10, Jeremiah is credited with prophesying that the Lord's betrayal price of the thirty pieces of silver would be given for the potter's field. One may search the entire prophecy of Jeremiah along with Lamentations and find no such statement. The only passage in Jeremiah's writings that even closely resembles this fulfillment is Jeremiah 18:1–4; 19:1–3. However, the connection is remote at best. Furthermore, the information found in Matthew seems to match up more accurately with Zechariah 11:12, 13 than with anything preserved in Jeremiah.

However, the entire seeming inaccuracy is cleared up by one word: spoken. Jeremiah spoke these words, but the Holy Spirit did not inspire him to write them down in his prophecy. At some point in Jeremiah's

125

ministry unknown to those in Jesus' day and just as mysterious to us today, Jeremiah preached a message in which he spoke these words. However, when the Lord dictated to Jeremiah what was to become inspired and preserved Scripture, this detail was not written.

Another such instance of this type of apparent inaccuracy is found in Acts 20:35 where the Lord Jesus is quoted as having said, "It is more blessed to give than to receive." One may search the Gospels and find many statements from the lips of Christ about giving and receiving, but this specific statement will not be found. In the Gospels, Christ is often found preaching or teaching on the topic of money and giving and receiving, but in none of those instances does He compare the blessedness of giving and receiving in the manner in which Acts 20:35 describes. Just as the issue of Jeremiah's words was cleared up, so this scenario becomes clear; and again, the clarity comes with just one word. This time, the word is said. Jesus Christ said this statement during his earthly ministry, but the Holy Ghost did not instruct Matthew, Mark, Luke, or John to write this quotation in his biographical account of Christ's earthly ministry. He instead waited and inspired Luke to write Paul's citation of these words of Christ in Acts.

In the spirit of John 20:30 and 21:25, both Jeremiah and the Lord Jesus Christ said and did many things not written. Jeremiah must have preached hundreds of messages that the Lord did not have him write down to be preserved for the text of Scripture. Jesus must have had countless conversations and taught innumerable lessons, given scores of parables and preached hundreds of messages not written down in Matthew, Mark, Luke, or John. Indeed, it is no stretch to assume that all of the Old Testament era prophets and all the New Testament era apostles said many things that were never written down. The conclusion is this: "But these are written, that ye might believe..." (John 20:31). What God had written down was to inculcate and cultivate belief. Is it not obvious that unbelievers, doubters and Scripture critics find reason not to believe based upon what is not written rather than delving into what is written and believing?

Quotations of Written Statements. Clarity necessitates that consideration also be given to the changes found in Old Testament statements and their New Testament counterparts. Many such examples can be cited, but perhaps a treatment of Psalm 40:6–8 and Hebrews 10:5–7 will serve to shed the light needed to understand this aspect.

Psalm 40:6–8 says, "Sacrifice and offering thou didst not desire; mine ears hast thou opened: burnt offering and sin offering hast thou not required. Then said I, Lo, I come: in the volume of the book it is written of me, I delight to do thy will, O my God: yea, thy law is within my heart." This portion was written by David just prior to the Battle of Ephraim as he hid from his son Absalom. David was testifying under Holy Ghost inspiration that God had opened his ears to truth and that he would obey rather than sacrifice. David was testifying of his willingness and desire to do God's will because God's law was within his heart.

Hebrews 10:5–7 says,

> "*Wherefore when he cometh into the world he saith, Sacrifice and offering thou wouldest not, but a body hast thou prepared me:*
> "*In burnt offerings and sacrifices for sin thou hast had no pleasure.*
> "*Then said I, Lo, I come (in the volume of the book it is written of me,) to do thy will, O God.*"

The author wrote here of Christ, of whom David was a spiritual type and physical ancestor. He spoke of Christ's understanding that his obedience unto death was required to fulfill all the sacrifices and offerings of the blood of bulls and lambs. Jesus submitted to God's will for him just as His earthly forebear David had done.

Several helpful ideas will help to defend the perfect accuracy of Scripture in cases such as this. Without unnecessary redundancy, the obvious first fact to consider is that the Author—well described in chapter one and well documented in chapter two—spoke both of these passages into the ears of holy men. The Author is "God only wise" (Romans 16:27). He had not forgotten what David wrote at the time when Hebrews was written. God had not changed his mind and given the author "corrections" or "improvements" of what David had written a millennium before. The Author, God of Creation and God of Salvation, has a right to restate Himself as many times and in as many variations as He chooses. He is God! He is the Author!

Again, Hebrews 10:5–7 is not a contradiction of Psalm 40:6–8 but a complement to it; Hebrews 10:5–7 is not a misrepresentation of Psalm 40:6–8 but an explanation of it. Modern-day translations are filled with

127

obvious contradictions and misrepresentations of the Masoretic Text of the Old Testament and the Textus Receptus of the New Testament. The Holy Ghost was completing the ideas of the Psalms passage when he authored the Hebrews portion. He was explaining the Psalm in Hebrews.

Third, note that Hebrews 10:5–7 is not a detraction from the original intention and expression of Psalm 40:6–8 but an application of that original intention and expression. Psalm 40:6–8 would have been limited to the experiences of David himself had the Lord not authorized their application also to the Messiah, the Son of David. Had not the Author brought that passage out of its immediate context of David's agonies during the rebellion of Absalom, no one would have known its meaning in connection with the Christ. It is at the Author's discretion that he lifted that passage higher than it had been before and placed it into the divine context of Jesus' agonies. The changes, authorized and divinely sanctioned, do not undermine or destroy. They build and glorify.

Fourth on this subject, please note that Hebrews 10:5–7 is not an arbitrary translation of Psalm 40:6–8; rather, it is an accurate revelation regarding Psalm 40:6–8. The Author God did not translate David's words to arrive at those in Hebrews. Rather, the Author was issuing forth additional revelation with regard to the referenced portion from David's writings.

In Exodus 6:2 and 3, "God spake unto Moses, and said unto him, I am the Lord: And I appeared unto Abraham, unto Isaac, and unto Jacob, by the name of God Almighty, but by my name JEHOVAH was I not known to them." All down through the centuries of Old Testament revelation, God made more and more known through similar examples of progressive revelation. In the New Testament, God continued that trend, and His words in Hebrews 10:5–7 are a reference to His words through David in Psalm 40:6–8, but they are also an enlargement of them, a clarifying of them, a solidifying of them.

Finally, and very importantly, Hebrews 10:5–7 is not a quotation of Psalm 40:6–8 for accuracy but a citation of that passage from the Psalm for authority. The difference between quotation for accuracy and citation for authority is enormous. The bulk of New Testament referencing to Old Testament writing is citation of the familiar to give credibility to the unfamiliar, citation of the text that had already been accepted to give reliability to the text that was to be added prior to the completion of the Scripture with the death of John the apostle.

Quotations of Absent Statements. Occasionally, the Word of God will indicate that a statement not found anywhere within its content is a citation. James 4:5 says, "Do ye think that the scripture saith in vain, The spirit that dwelleth in us lusteth to envy?" Avid Bible students may search the Old and New Testament text in vain to find this statement elsewhere in Scripture. Not even a close rendition exists. Concordance searches of the main words of the verse will not yield fruit.

What, then, does God mean when He says that the Scripture says something that one cannot find written in any other Scripture? Here, God the Author makes a broad, sweeping statement. It is as if the Lord is saying that His overall message in Scripture teaches that man's spirit lusts to envy. Certainly, much is said in both Old and New Testament books about the unregenerate spirit. Much is also said in both testaments about the regenerate spirit that is not in tune with God's indwelling Spirit. James, under inspiration of the Holy Ghost, is asking if his readers think that God's overall message about the condition of man's spirit is spoken in vain.

Bible correctors and multiversionists revel in such situations as these because they compare their arbitrary changing of Scripture to accommodate their culture and increase their sales to the Lord's authoritative development of Scripture to accomplish its completion and communicate full truth. There is no comparison. Bible changers are not the Bible's Author! Case closed.

Absolute Truth and Numbers. Numbering is a common subject where Satan and his representatives are wont, with calumnious slanders, to cast the Bible onto the heap of inaccuracy. This writer believes that the numbers of people, years and things as recorded in the Bible are absolutely and accurately true. There is no temporary truth or approximate truth unless the context clearly states so.

Joshua 8:12 tells the reader that Joshua "took about five thousand men, and set them to lie in ambush between Beth-el and Ai." John 6:10 reveals that when Jesus was about to break the bread and fish,

129

He commanded His disciples to have the people sit down, and "the men sat down, in number about five thousand." Acts 4:4 speaks of a moment when Peter had preached, and "many of them which heard the word believed; and the number of the men was about five thousand." Obvious to these texts is the approximation of the number, but not of the truth. God said "about five thousand" in each instance. The absolute truth is that there were about five thousand men in each of these familiar biblical accounts. No honest student of Scripture will attempt to explain away the closeness to five thousand by lame efforts that claim that ancient methods of reckoning and counting were different than ours, or that the absence of vowels in Hebrew makes numbers hard to render, or that glorified statistics made for better miracles!

The Old Testament gives amazingly short times for creation and amazingly long life spans for the patriarchs, especially prior to the flood of Noah. Much effort has been made by gap theorists and other Bible critics to explain that the days of the Creation week were really ages and that the lives of the patriarchs were calculated using different "years" than what we use today.

Truthfully and accurately, God spoke this world and all its terrestrial and celestial counterparts into existence out of nothing, and it took him only the time span of six spoken statements beginning with the word let. Those spoken statements took place on consecutive twenty-four-hour days "in the beginning" (Genesis 1:1; John 1:1). Truthfully and accurately, Methusaleh lived on this planet Earth for nine hundred sixty-nine years. Each of those years had three hundred sixty-five days, and each of those days had twenty-four hours!

Reigns of kings and ages at which they ascended their thrones and then passed away have long been the subject of the absolute accuracy debate. Again, while there may be some confusion between accounts in Kings versus Chronicles, those seeming difficulties are ironed out quite easily when one gives more credit to the Holy Spirit and less credit to the detractors! Even the favorite numbering question, the age of Ahaziah at his ascension to the throne of Judah, is absolutely accurate and can be figured out with careful study and honest comparisons. One writer calls this supposed difficulty the "Gordian Knot of the Chronology of the Kings of Israel and Judah," but let it be remembered that

130

even the Gordian knot was cut by the sword of Alexander the Great.

The number of horses that Solomon had (four thousand or forty thousand?) and the number of times the cock crowed before Peter denied the Lord (one or two?) and all other such seeming discrepancies are actually accurate when read and studied in their contexts and considered in light of all other details in the supposedly inaccurate accounts.

Absolute Truth and People and Places. The numerous names of people in the Bible have overlap just like the names of places. King Solomon was also known as Jedidiah (II Samuel 12:25) and may also be the person known as Lemuel in Proverbs 31. Moses' father-in-law Jethro was also known by the name Hobab. Phalec and Peleg refer to the same person. Jehoiakim is also known as Eliakim, and his son Jehoiachin was also called Coniah and Jeconiah or Jeconias, depending upon which account one is reading. King David's second son was known as Chileab and as Daniel. Peter's given name was Simon, but the Lord called him Cephas, and James called him Simeon. Such instances as these could bring a person to cast aspersion upon the accuracy of the Bible, but the truth found there is absolute.

Most of the apparent difficulties regarding places can be explained when one realizes that places often have more than one name. Consider that Egypt is also known as Mizraim, Phut and Put; that the names Babylon, Chaldea and Ur are used interchangeably; that Israel is also called Palestina, Palestine and Ephraim to name a few; and that Jerusalem is called Salem, Jebus, the city of David, and Zion. Another problem about places is that one name may refer to more than one specific or general location. Zion, for instance, refers to Jerusalem and to Heaven. Two Bethlehems and two Antiochs are cited in Scripture.

These are not unreasonable concepts. This author's present circle of influence has given him more than one title or name and has caused him to cross paths with several individuals with the same first name, with the same initials and with the same last name. He currently resides in LaGrange, Indiana, but a search of Wikipedia will show about twenty states that have a place called La Grange. The accuracy of the Bible is no more threatened by these person-name and place-name situations than this writer's personal identity or location is jeopardized by other people or places with the same name.

Whatever the Bible addresses, it addresses accurately. Without a doubt, the words "No Cross-Examination Needed" could be penned upon its spine.

13

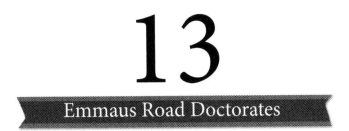

Emmaus Road Doctorates

The correct response to liberal intellectualism and neo-evangelical pseudo-spirituality is fundamental scholarship, not fundamental ignorance. Altogether too many of the speakers and writers on the subjects of inspiration and preservation are poorly educated, and some actually convey a disdain for learning as if learning itself is responsible for—or much worse, equivalent to—apostasy. While the cause of apostasy and unbelief often finds roots in the religious intelligentsia, it is not educational training per se that is responsible for apostasy; rather, apostasy and apostate thinking are responsible for the wrong applications of education. In short, many doctorates both of the earned and of the honorary type are granted to ones with swollen heads and shriveled hearts.

Quite honestly, there are also many faithful stewards of God's Word who have served in small corners of the Lord's vineyard with integrity and humility who are truly worthy of a doctorate. Just as sure is the fact that there are worthy recipients, and there are worthy schools honoring graduates with honorary doctorates. Therefore, it is necessary to identify that this is not a knock against education or degrees; neither is this an effort to scrap the preacher who has not received multiple degrees. This is primarily a warning against mail-order doctorates and donated dignities that satisfy intellectualistic greed and portray a level of academia that has never been achieved.

Intellectualism is the enemy of inspiration and of preservation as well. Intellectualism and all its collaborators and corroborators stand in opposition to the miracles of inspiration and preservation of the Word of God. Without rudeness or malice, it must be asserted that the mainline denominationalists, the nondenominationalists, and the interdenominationalists of our day are almost exclusively intellectual-istic in their approaches to Bible study. The writers and speakers from these camps approach the study of Scripture from the premise that there must of necessity be mistakes due to human error on the part of the copyists and translators.

Mainline denominationalists have a doctrine of tradition above truth, and most of those adhering to traditionalist Methodism, Congregationalism or Presbyterianism (for example) are mired in the bogs of theological argumentation about Calvinism, Arminianism and a host of other isms and schisms to no avail other than "the subverting of the hearers" (II Timothy 2:14). The nondenominationalists have no doctrine except for a personal statement that is so nebulous it could be agreeable to anyone. The interdenominationalists have a doctrine but will "lovingly" lay it aside for the sake of unity of all denominations; they believe their doctrine in their hearts but won't impose said belief systems upon anyone. In such mainline, non-, or inter- circles, a changeable Bible thrives because intellectualism corresponds to an evolving, flexible doctrine and the ethic it fosters.

Opposing Approaches to the Majesty, Mystery and Might of Scripture. The intellectualist rises above each verse of the Scripture and judges it to be accurate or inaccurate, well translated or poorly translated, necessary or unnecessary, part of the narrative or not. Indeed, the intellectualist even digs down to the individual words of the verses, deeming from his supposedly superior stance whether or not that word is pertinent, understandable enough, exact, or appropriate. The inspirationist on the other hand believes by faith that the exact words are unchangeable, and that the changing should occur in the heart of the reader, not in the material read. Inspirationists accept by faith that the God of Heaven breathed the words; that the Holy Ghost oversaw the copying and translation of accurate texts into accurate translations; and that while no second work of inspiration occurred, inspiration was not sacrificed by the copying or translation.

Opposing Appreciations for the Merit of Scripture. To the intellectualist, the Bible is a money-making bestseller on the cutting edge of new information. As soon as the sales begin to drop, another new and improved version must be produced to augment the money flow and satisfy the insatiable appetites of worldlings for something never heard or seen before. Inspirationists see the Bible as owned and copyrighted by God the Father—not a stylish publication for financial profiteering, but the very words of the very God of Heaven for spiritual profit in doctrine, reproof, correction, and instruction in righteousness, "that the man of God may be perfect, throughly furnished unto all good works" (II Timothy 3:17).

Opposing Applications of the Message of Scripture. By and large, the intellectualists believe and teach an overall figurative and par-abolical—if not mythical—application of the general message of the Bible. Inspirationists, however, believe and teach a literal application of the exact message of God's Word, settling for a figurative or parabolical understanding only when both text and context require it. Inspirationists use the adage "when literal sense makes perfect sense, seek no other sense."

When Jesus addressed the disciples on the Emmaus Road following His resurrection, He began "at Moses and all the prophets [and] expounded unto them in all the scriptures the things concerning himself" (Luke 24:27). After Jesus' sudden disappearance from their home, these two disciples exclaimed, "Did not our heart burn within us, while he talked with us by the way, and while he opened to us the scriptures?" (Luke 24:32). Later that evening, as those two disciples reported to the other disciples back in Jerusalem that they had seen the resurrected Lord and conversed with him, "Jesus himself stood in the midst of them...And he said unto them, These are the words which I spake unto you, while I was yet with you, that all things must be fulfilled, which were written in the law of Moses, and in the prophets, and in the psalms, concerning [himself]" (Vss. 36, 44). No wonder the very next verse says, "Then opened he their understanding, that they might understand the scriptures" (vs. 45).

Jesus Christ, the Master Teacher, gave the Emmaus disciples and the eleven a complete overview from what was, at that time, the three major sections of Scripture: law, prophecy and poetry. Having heard from the lips of the Saviour who was Himself the direct fulfillment of the prophecies of which He spoke, those disciples suddenly had great and open understanding! They received their Emmaus Road "doctorates" from

135

none other than the Lord Jesus Christ.

In this age of grace, any complete study of any Scripture topic other than mysteries not revealed in the Old Testament (such as the church) must include truth from the Law, the Prophets and the poetical books, as well as from the New Testament. (See Chapter Two.) Given this four-section foundation for study and understanding, one should be able to find soundly applied verses of Scripture about the inspiration and preservation of Scripture from the Law, the Prophets, the Poetry, and the New Testament. And indeed one can find those passages.

The Law. In what is commonly called the Law or the Pentateuch (Genesis, Exodus, Leviticus, Numbers, and Deuteronomy), God gave several direct statements about the inspiration and preservation of His Word. That the Law is inspired, that is, given directly by God, is averred repeatedly. Seventy-four times in those five books, one can read the words "the Lord spake unto Moses, saying." What is this if it is not divine inspiration, the God of Heaven speaking directly from His mouth to Moses' ear?

But did God speak in the Law about preservation? Yes, he did. The Book of Deuteronomy is Moses' final discourse to God's people prior to his Home-going. Repeatedly, Moses references "the land which the Lord sware unto your fathers" (Deuteronomy 1:8), and in all but one of these specific instances, he is instructing the new generation regarding their responsibility to carry out the exact commands of God once they would inhabit the land. It would literally be impossible for the children of Israel to carry out at some point in the future the commands which Moses had given in the past unless God preserved those commands in the hands of copyists.

Therefore, it is no surprise that God said,

> "Now therefore hearken, O Israel, unto the statutes and unto the judgments, which I teach you, for to do them, that ye may live, and go in and possess the land which the LORD God of your fathers giveth you.
> "Ye shall not add unto the word which I command you, neither shall ye diminish ought from it, that ye may keep the commandments of the LORD your God which I command you."—Deuteronomy 4:1, 2.

Again, he said "What thing soever I command you, observe to do it: thou shalt not add thereto, nor diminish from it" (Deuteronomy

12:32). It would not have been possible for the people to keep the commandments of the Lord if words, ideas or precepts were added or deleted from what God said. In order for these two specific commands of Moses from the lips of the Holy Ghost to have any meaning at all to the new generation and to ensuing generations of Israelites, what He had said previously had to have been preserved perfectly for those future generations.

The Prophets. For the prophets, many voices sounded the trumpet of inspiration and preservation, even as there are many prophetic voices. Scripture cites both speaking and writing prophets with some overlap. For instance, Elisha and Elisha were speaking prophets without books of the Bible bearing their names. Jeremiah and Micah were writing prophets who both spoke and wrote down selected passages from their speaking ministries as the Holy Ghost moved upon them to do.

In the first chapter of his glorious and notable prophecies, Jeremiah recorded the details of his call into public ministry. According to Jeremiah 1:6 and well-studied Bible chronologies, Jeremiah was likely about twelve years of age when God put his hand upon him and began to speak through him in the public venues of Jerusalem at large as people traversed the marketplaces and specifically in the temple gate as the worshipers came with their sacrifices and went away again.

Opening his collection of written prophecies as he did, Jeremiah recorded specific words from God that give irrefutable evidence of inspiration. God said, "Whatsoever I command thee thou shalt speak... Behold, I have put my words in thy mouth...Thou therefore gird up thy loins, and arise, and speak unto them all that I command thee" (Jeremiah 1:7, 9, 17). When God said to his servant, "I will utter my judgments" (v.16), he was telling Jeremiah that at a time yet future, he would put words of judgment into Jeremiah's mouth.

Multiple times in the fifty-two chapters of the preserved compilation of Jeremiah's works, he writes, "The word of the Lord came to me...,"or, "The word of the Lord that came to Jeremiah." It was not Jeremiah's word. It was God's Word, spoken from God's mouth into Jeremiah's ear and out through Jeremiah's mouth into the ears of disobedient and rebellious Judah.

In his poignant sermon against the faithless shepherds, God gave

Jeremiah truth on the subject of inspiration from the other side. In words unrivaled even in Scripture text, God thundered against the entire concept of intellectualistic supposition as to the message of God. The only positive thing from the lips of the Lord in this entire passage addresses the prophet who has God's Word and speaks it faithfully.

> "I have heard what the prophets said, that prophesy lies in my name, saying, I have dreamed, I have dreamed.
>
> "How long shall this be in the heart of the prophets that prophesy lies? yea, they are prophets of the deceit of their own heart;
>
> "Which think to cause my people to forget my name by their dreams which they tell every man to his neighbour, as their fathers have forgotten my name for Baal.
>
> "The prophet that hath a dream, let him tell a dream; and he that hath my word, let him speak my word faithfully. What is the chaff to the wheat? saith the Lord.
>
> "Is not my word like as a fire? saith the Lord; and like a hammer that breaketh the rock in pieces?
>
> "Therefore, behold, I am against the prophets, saith the Lord, that steal my words every one from his neighbour.
>
> "Behold, I am against the prophets, saith the Lord, that use their tongues, and say, He saith.
>
> "Behold, I am against them that prophesy false dreams, saith the Lord, and do tell them, and cause my people to err by their lies, and by their lightness; yet I sent them not, nor commanded them: therefore they shall not profit this people at all, saith the Lord"—Jeremiah 23:25–32.

Even the lost world around Jeremiah understood that he spoke God's truth. Perhaps the most rebellious of Jeremiah's contemporaries was King Zedekiah, but even he asked the prophet, "Is there any word from the Lord?" (Jeremiah 37:17). He did not ask, "Jeremiah, what do you say?" or "Jeremiah, what is your take on present-day affairs?" He asked the prophet what the message of God was about the matters of political and military import to the remnant of the people under his tottering puppet leadership.

As to preservation, Jeremiah spoke emphatically and authoritatively. One example occurs in Jeremiah 11:1–8 in the middle of his message on the broken covenant. The covenant to which God referred in this passage was that which God had commanded in the day He brought them forth out of the land of Egypt. The people had but to obey His voice and do the commands in order to be His people and for Him to be their God.

Interestingly, Jeremiah was faulting his present generation for not obeying and performing those commands. One must ask at this juncture how it would have been possible for people in Jeremiah's day to be held accountable for living in accord with a covenant that was some eight centuries old unless that covenant had been perfectly preserved so that they could know it! How could God be angry enough to pronounce through Jeremiah a curse upon the inhabitants of Judah unless that covenant had been preserved perfectly so that they had it in their possession and were therefore accountable? Evident beyond doubt is the fact that faithful copyists had painstakingly written out the words of Moses book by book, word for word, letter for letter. Jeremiah's generation had the words of God through Moses as much as Moses' and Joshua's generations had them because God preserved them!

Moreover, God did not hold Jeremiah's generaton responsible for the general ideas or basic message of what Moses had written at the mouth of God. Oh no. Rather, the people of Jerusalem and Judah in the days of Jeremiah the prophet were held to the standard of "all the words of this covenant, which [God] commanded them to do; but they did them not" (v. 8).

Farther along in Jeremiah's ministry, as he ministered one day in the court of the Lord's house in the beginning of the reign of Jehoiakim, God told Jeremiah to speak the whole message, the entire message. Then he said, "Diminish not a word" (26:2). As Jeremiah proceeded to scold the apostates who chanted their hypocritical mantras in the temple court, he likened that temple and its superficial worshipers to the worshipers at Shiloh in the days of Eli, Hophni and Phineas. Such words of cutting-edge truth disturbed the priests and false prophets to the point they threatened Jeremiah with death. Jeremiah's response in Jeremiah 26:12–15 is a preservationist's gold mine. The mighty prophet told his audience so dull of hearing, "The Lord sent me to prophesy against this house and against this city all the words that ye have heard…for of a truth the Lord hath sent me unto you to speak all these words in your ears." Twice he affirms that he was sent with "all" the words. Jeremiah was not diminishing anything, not even one word.

Jeremiah 29:1 makes another strong case for preservation in the writings of the prophet. Jeremiah had sent a letter from Jerusalem to the Jews of the first captivity who had been taken to Babylon some nine years before. Elasah the son of Shaphan and Gemariah the son of Hilkiah had carried this letter from Jerusalem to Babylon. Nine years having elapsed, Jeremiah wrote down "the words of the letter" in his collection of preserved writings. He did not write down the basic idea, a general idea or a similar idea. He wrote the words, meaning exact words, of that letter which he had sent to a foreign city and which was now in the possession of those to whom it had been written in that city. Such an instance requires the oversight of God to preserve his word in its exactness.

What a powerful rebuke to the nonpreservationist view that this or that word or words can be arbitrarily deleted based upon a consensus of scholars or an isolated variant manuscript or two! God held a different opinion of preservation of His Word in the seventh century before Christ, and He yet holds that position, namely, that every word is important. God made no allowance in Jeremiah's day for either an eclectic or a dynamic equivalency approach to His divinely inspired word; nor does He make such allowance now. It is the intellectuals who wish to relegate God's specific words to an approximate message derived by comparisons between multiple contradictory manuscripts. Inspirationists and preservationists maintain that God oversaw the entire process; furthermore, they aver that contradictory manuscripts are the work of unfaithful copyists and scribes whose agenda in Jeremiah's day was little different than is the agenda of the multiversionists of the twenty-first century!

Jeremiah is not isolated in his teachings on inspiration and preservation. Ezekiel, who follows Jeremiah both in the order of Bible writers and in the chronological presentation of Jewish history, gives amazing truth regarding these same issues. Forty-seven times in the book that bears his name, Ezekiel writes, "The word of the Lord came," and this is but one of the ways Ezekiel tells us that God was the source of his prophecies.

The Psalms (Poetry). Scholars may differ slightly regarding the classification of poetic Scripture. All conservative writers include Job,

Psalms, Proverbs, Ecclesiastes, and Song of Solomon (called Canticles in some Bibles published in the early 1900s and prior). Some fundamentalists also include in this category the Book of Lamentations. A few might even classify some of the more fluid portions found in the writings of the prophets under the heading of poetry. Regardless of the specific classifications, the poetry of God's precious Word yields further revelation about inspiration and preservation.

A favorite passage from the Psalms is Psalm 12:6, 7 where God promises to preserve His Word from the generation in which it was first written for ever. That "the words of the Lord are pure words" should suffice to let mankind know that they are unique, sanctified and, therefore, the object of some specific attention from God worthy of the specific attention of man. That specific attention from God is that they resemble "silver tried in a furnace of earth, purified seven times." Poetic meaning of the number seven is perfection. God literally speaks words that are pure to perfection. Why would God who speaks words that are pure to the realm of perfection then abandon those words to the careless and inappreciative among men so that they could dilute them or discard them? The obvious answer is that He hasn't.

The next statement of the verses is a bold declaration that God would keep and preserve them "from this generation for ever." David's use of the words this generation referred to the generation in which he lived, the generation in which the words were given by inspiration. David's subsequent reference to for ever is a literal term. And the last time this writer checked, "for ever" meant "for ever". Furthermore, upon further examination, "for ever" has not yet ended.

The context of these two verses is also significant. The entire Psalm is about a contrast between the words of men and the words of God. David solicits the help of God because of the ceasing of the godly and the faithful from among the general population of men (v. 1). In the societal place of godly and faithful men were vain men who spoke with flattery and duplicity (v. 2), with pride and presumption (v. 3, 4), with oppressive bravado (v. 5), and with vile wickedness (v. 8). Therefore, contextually, the pure (inspired) and kept (preserved) words of God are contrasted with sinners' words that are neither pure nor notable!

It is exegetical fraud to attempt to purport that these two verses are not intended to teach inspiration and preservation. The hocus pocus chicanery of multiversionists is powerless against the plain statement of God in the plain context of this Psalm.

Psalms 19 and 119

Psalm 19 and 119 are two treasure troves for the inspiration-ist/preservationist position. In both psalms, God references His Law, testimony, commandments, statutes, judgments, and ways. Psalm 19 teaches that these specific types of Scripture statement are "more to be desired...than much fine gold," a beautifully poetic statement with definitely literal meaning. The Word of God is more valuable than the gold of Ophir.

In the nineteenth Psalm, David continues under inspiration to say that these specific types of Scripture statement serve to warn God's servants and to reward those who keep them. How can any servant of God beyond the generation of King David be warned if the inspired warnings themselves are not preserved but are changed, expanded or deleted? How can any servant of the Lord after the time of the son of Jesse be rewarded by keeping such inspired laws, commandments, etc., if indeed they are not preserved but are altered, added to or taken from?

While the obvious theme of Psalm 19 is the Word of God in general, the focus of verses 7–11 just as evidently implies both inspiration and preservation. Again, only a system of hermeneutical spoof would deny that what King David wrote in his day some three millennia ago can have no power at all in our present generation unless the God who gave the Word also preserved it.

It is almost literary overkill to cite Psalm 119 which this author believes to have been written by Ezra as a psalm of the restoration period. Having been long affected by Babylonian idolatry during the captivity, the Jewish remnant needed assurance with regard to the Scripture, and this psalm accomplishes that with finesse and finality. Some aspect of God's Word is treated in almost every one of its one hundred seventy-six verses. Some of Ezra the priest's statements are so bold and clear that one would need to be a hermeneutical illusionist to refuse his preservationist position. And well did Ezra establish at the close of the Old Testament canon the importance of preservation! With only the Book of Malachi being penned after Psalm 119, Ezra the priest, the scribe, was giving in this unmatched psalm the necessary truth of preservation even as the four-centuries-long "famine…of hearing the words of the Lord" (Amos 8:11) approached and as "the sun [went] down over the prophets (Micah 3:6). For the four centuries after the death of Ezra the priest in the latter half of the 400s B.C.., no voice of God was given. Indeed, just as was said of God's revelation in the last days of the tabernacle's resting at Shiloh, "the word of the Lord was precious in those days; there was no open vision" (I Samuel 3:1).

To give much-needed assurance to the struggling remnant of faithful believers through those centuries of silence while they awaited the day when God would "shake all nations, and the desire of all nations [would] come" (Haggai 2:7), God inspired Ezra to write that there would be one thing that would last, and that would be the Scripture.

While it would be possible to cite every reference to preservation in Psalm 119, it is unnecessary. Suffice it to say that preservation is clear in the words of several verses. Consider the many times that Ezra claimed he had kept God's commands, laws, testimonies, etc. (vss. 2, 4, 5, 8, 17, 22, 33, 34, 44, 55, 56, 57, 60, 63, 67, 69, 88, 100, 101, 106, 115, 129, 134, 136, 145, 146, 158, 167 and 168). Such confident statements would have been mere fleshly boasts unless God had preserved His Word from all the writers since Job and Moses so that Ezra could not only keep them but also know he had kept them!

Also found in the poetry section of the Old Testament text is Proverbs 22:12, an interesting and seldom cited verse in the inspiration and preservation debate. While the methods of inspiration are clear in Scripture, the method or methods of preservation are primarily taken for granted. God has made blanket statements that His Word is preserved—period. He has not made His methods or manner of preservation known. However, God gave Solomon a hint about preservation methodology when He inspired him to write, "The eyes of the Lord preserve knowledge, and he overthroweth the words of the transgressor."

The two verses prior to Proverbs 22:12 mention scorners and those who love pureness of heart. Obviously, scorners are those who despise God's Word. Within the context of Proverbs, the scorner is defined as one who "heareth not rebuke" (13:1); "seeketh wisdom, and findeth it not (14:6); "loveth not one that reproveth him" (15:12); "dealeth in proud wrath" (21:24); and "is an abomination to men" (24:9). A scorner does not hear rebuke because he does not listen to God's Word. He does not find wisdom because he rejects the source and fountain of wisdom, the Word of God. He does not love his reprovers because his reprovers use the very Scripture to which he refuses to listen. He deals in proud wrath along with all others who reject the Bible. He is an abomination to men because the very fabric of his soul is woven with rejection of God's eternal truth.

Those who are pure in heart, however, are the ones who love the Scriptures. "Blessed are the pure in heart: for they shall see God" (Matthew 5:8). Where does one better see God than in the inspired, preserved Word of God? Solomon's father wrote in Psalm 24:3 and 4 that the one who ascends into the hill of the Lord and stands in the holy place is one who "hath clean hands, and a pure heart; who hath not lifted up his soul unto vanity, nor sworn deceitfully." Who, more than those who love and defend the perfect Scriptures, can be described as not having lifted up their souls to vanity?

How amazing, then, is this proverb! The eyes of the Lord that "are in every place, beholding the evil and the good" (Proverbs 15:3) are the same eyes that preserve His knowledge. The eyes of the Lord which are known to "run to and fro throughout the whole earth, to shew himself strong in the behalf of them whose heart is perfect toward him" (II Chronicles 16:9) are the same eyes that preserve His knowledge. God's knowledge is preserved by His all-seeing, all-watchful, all-attentive, all-concerned eye. If God is able to watch and attend His sainted souls amid the teeming throngs of six inhabited continents and "deliver [them] from every evil work, and…preserve [them] unto his heavenly kingdom" (II Timothy 4:18), most surely He can watch and attend His own precious Word and deliver it from every evil work and preserve it forever!

If God overthrows the words of the transgressor, that would be the perverse and the ungodly words, not the pure words of Scripture. The knowledge which His eyes preserve must be the eternal spiritual knowledge found in Scripture, indeed, the very Word and words that He inspired. God preserves His own knowledge by the simple means of ensuring that there are always faithful scribes to copy it exactly, the simple means of filling humble men with a yearning to translate it honestly, and the simple means of guarding its presence in clay jars and urns in caves for centuries of time. Our great God is well able to do that.

The New Testament. So common are the citations of II Timothy 3:16, 17 and II Peter 1:20, 21 that some people want simply to wave the hand and seek some new angle; however, those two venerable portions are pillars upon which and between which hang the suspension bridge of all New Testament inspiration and preservation truth. The Timothy and Peter portions are New Testament declarations of inspiration. The process of God's inspiring the Apostles by giving truth from His very mouth into the very ears of holy men of God and by moving them to write exact and specific words at His bidding is nowhere more clearly proposed.

However, the New Testament is not poverty stricken for more than these two familiar portions of truth about the inspiration-preservation issue. The balance of this chapter is devoted to examination of some less often cited New Testament Scriptures on the subject. This will familiarize each reader with the fact that the position of inspiration and preservation of the King James Bible for English-speaking souls is well documented in the New Testament.

Room and time need to be given first to the fact that the "second" Epistles (II Corinthians, II Thessalonians, II Timothy, II Peter, and II John) all deal in some manner and to some degree with the concept of corruption of the Scriptures that were known in apostolic times. Jude also deals with this theme, and it is notable that Jude might have written two letters, because he "gave all diligence to write…of the common salvation" (vs. 3), but God was urgent upon him to write a contention for the faith instead which could have been II Jude if Jude had been permitted and inspired to write I Jude about the common salvation. The fact that so much space is given in second Epistles to the theme of corruption of the Scripture is important to the inspiration-preservation cause. Truly, just as quickly as first Epistles were written, attempts were made to change, add to and subtract from them so that the Holy Spirit had to make note of those attempts in the second Epistles.

II Corinthians. Paul's fivefold mention of Satan by name in the Corinthian epistles is not surprising, considering the carnality of the members of that local assembly and the Devil's close proximity to and involvement with that type of believers. Three of those five citations are in II Corinthians, and in II Corinthians 11:13–15, the apostle Paul identifies one of the chief methods of Scripture manuscript corruption: Satan's ministers posing as apostles of truth. According to Holy Ghost direction, however, Paul identified them as "false apostles, deceitful workers," who, at the direction of "Satan himself [who] is transformed into an angel of light," seek to deceive. No doubt these were on Paul's mind when he wrote of "many, which corrupt the word of God" (II Corinthians 2:17).

What is generally overlooked in this connection is that hard on the heels of this stark exposure of the Devil and his heinous attempts to thwart the truth through the poseurs of affected righteousness, Satan also assays to cripple the true apostles. Chapter twelve gives the Bible reader both a comforting and a sobering truth: "There was given to [Paul] a thorn in the flesh, the messenger of Satan to buffet [him]" (12:7). And for what reason was this thorny messenger sent to buffet the true apostle? Simply put, the Devil sought to trouble and cripple the true apostle because of "the abundance of the revelations," that is, revelations of truth given by inspiration to Paul. The true apostle thus exposed the Devil's treachery against the New Testament Scripture. Satan was propping up wax figures and chopping down the real man. All of that was an attempt to discredit the messenger of truth and disannul the message of truth. This was a grand plot to destroy the truth, but it did not work, because God overcame Satan's immediate plan by giving Paul sufficient grace and overran Satan's ultimate plan by preserving the truths given to Paul in his Epistles in the New Testament.

In this Epistle that serves as the Holy-Spirit-inspired defense of his apostleship, Paul wrote, "For we are not as many, which corrupt the word of God: but as of sincerity, but as of God, in the sight of God speak we in Christ...[and] have renounced the hidden things of dishonesty, not walking in craftiness, nor handling the word of God deceitfully; but by manifestation of the truth commending ourselves to every man's conscience in the sight of God" (II Corinthians 2:17; 4:2). Such statements, given as they are by God Himself, require that there were those in Paul's day who were corrupting the Word of God, who were not sincere, who were speaking without the authority and filling of Christ, who were involved in dishonest and crafty practice, and who were handling God's Word in deceitful manner.

Paul, on the other hand, was not involved in that corrupting process. His Spirit-inspired words here would be inane unless Paul had been one of the chief spokesmen for Holy-Ghost-preserved truth. He could not have made any claim that his words were a manifestation of the truth to the consciences of men in the sight of God had he not been preaching truth long preserved and kept in the purity of its original message. While Paul certainly preached to his Corinthian audiences the "wisdom of God in a mystery" (I Corinthians 2:7), and while that mystery "from the beginning of the world ha[d] been hid in God" (Ephesians 3:9), he also filled his preaching with Old Testament truth as is seen in even a cursory study of his messages found in the Book of Acts. The Old Testament truths he preached were among the concepts he cited when he told the Corinthians that he spoke in Christ. Those Old Testament truths, then, had to have been preserved for him to preach to them.

II Timothy; Titus. One of the starkest and most profound New Testament passages on preservation is found in II Timothy 1:13,14. There, Paul wrote under inspiration, "Hold fast the form of sound words, which thou hast heard of me, in faith and love which is in Christ Jesus. That good thing which was committed unto thee keep by the Holy Ghost which dwelleth in us." The "form of sound words" that Timothy was to "hold fast" was the maintaining of the proper usage of the exact words of Scripture. "That good thing which was committed" was most certainly not his salvation. It was the glorious Scripture committed into his trust. Paul enjoined his young preacher boy to guard that treasure by the power of the indwelling Holy Ghost!

As Paul wrote to his "preacher boys," he was wont to urge them on in strong positions, and that makes it quite natural for him to list among requirements for an ordained elder/bishop (i.e. pastor) in the local church that he be one capable of "holding fast the faithful word as he hath been taught, that he may be able by sound doctrine both to exhort and to convince the gainsayers" (Titus 1:9). Such a statement that names the faithful word implies that, even in the days of Paul and Titus, there was an unfaithful word, that is, a corrupted text, as seen in earlier chapters of this book. While it has been noted that God said little in

Scripture about His methods of preservation, another hint is found here. The godly pastors were to be men who would know the faithful word and hold it fast! That faithful word is the uncorrupted text that proposes sound doctrine that is effective in repudiating the gainsayers who preach and teach the unfaithful word. Were there no preservation of God's Word, or if God did not use human instruments in his work of preservation (as he does in other works such as evangelism and edification), such a leadership requirement as is listed in Titus 1:9 would be moot and irrelevant.

In Paul's great treatise to the Ephesians, the Holy Spirit inspired the apostle to write that the local, corporate church of Jesus Christ and the saints individually are

> "Fellowcitizens with the saints, and of the household of God;
> "And are built upon the foundation of the apostles and prophets, Jesus Christ himself being the chief corner stone;
> "In whom all the building fitly framed together groweth unto an holy temple in the Lord:
> "In whom ye also are builded together for an habitation of God through the Spirit"—Ephesians 2:19–22.

What a gold mine of preservation is found here! If the apostles and prophets and Christ himself were the foundation and cornerstone upon which the church at Ephesus was built, then the truth those prophets had written centuries earlier and the words Christ had spoken a generation earlier had to be preserved somewhere for those saints.

Furthermore, if, as we believe, the local, corporate churches of the twenty-first century and the individual saints within their memberships are also built upon that foundation and cornerstone, then the words of the apostles must be added to that list of preserved words. It is ludicrous to believe that the foundation and cornerstone are secure but that the wall and building are "daubed...with untempered morter" (Ezekiel 13:10) yet still stand. Ezekiel wrote that the structure built with untempered morter

> "shall fall: there shall be an overflowing shower; and ye, O great hailstones, shall fall; and a stormy wind shall rend it.
> "Lo, when the wall is fallen, shall it not be said unto you, Where is the daubing wherewith ye have daubed it?"

> *"So will I break down the wall that ye have daubed with untempered morter, and bring it down to the ground, so that the foundation thereof shall be discovered, and it shall fall."*
>
> *"Thus will I accomplish my wrath upon the wall, and upon them that have daubed it with untempered morter, and will say unto you, The wall is no more, neither they that daubed it"*—Vss. 11, 12, 14, 15.

This sounds quite different from the house that Jesus described in Matthew 7:24, 25 that stood because it was built upon the rock of His truth and obedience to that truth.

II Peter. When Peter wrote "to the strangers scattered throughout Pontus, Galatia, Cappadocia, Asia, and Bithynia" (I Peter 1:1), he launched into salvation doctrine, mentioning such glories as the sprinkled blood of Jesus Christ, the lively hope by the resurrection of Christ, the keeping power of God through faith, and the precious trials of one's faith. In his declaration, he addressed "salvation ready to be revealed in the last time" and "the end of your faith, even the salvation of your souls" (vss. 5, 9). Then, Peter said this salvation was a mysterious marvel regarding which

> *"The prophets have inquired and searched diligently, who prophesied of the grace that should come unto you:*
>
> *"Searching what, or what manner of time the Spirit of Christ which was in them did signify, when it testified beforehand the sufferings of Christ, and the glory that should follow.*
>
> *"Unto whom it was revealed, that not unto themselves, but unto us they did minister the things, which are now reported unto you by them that have preached the gospel unto you with the Holy Ghost sent down from heaven; which things the angels desire to look into"*—Vss. 10–12.

One preacher said this grand salvation was prophet-inquired, Spirit-inspired and angel-desired. What a salvation! But look at what God said here. He said the prophets did not fully comprehend the timing aspect of God's salvation plan. They "inquired and searched diligently" as to what the Holy Spirit signified (meant) when He spoke through them of the initial suffering and eventual glory of Christ. However, even though they did not grasp God's calendar, they did understand one thing, and that was that they were not ministering to themselves but unto future generations. This is a forceful passage for inspiration because of the clear statement that the Spirit of Christ signified truth and testified of that truth through the prophets. Just as forceful, however, is this passage on the subject of preservation because the prophets who wrote from 1500 to 400 B.C. could not possibly have ministered to future generations if their writings were to fall into corruption and decay and not be preserved for those future generations.

This chapter, however, does not stop handling the subject of inspiration and preservation here. After several exhortations and commands in verses 13–22, Peter returns to the preservation issue when he says,

> "Being born again, not of corruptible seed, but of incorruptible, by the word of God, which liveth and abideth for ever.
> "For all flesh is as grass, and all the glory of man as the flower of grass. The grass withereth, and the flower thereof falleth away:
> "But the word of the Lord endureth for ever. And this is the word which by the gospel is preached unto you.
> "Wherefore laying aside all malice, and all guile, and hypocrisies, and envies, and all evil speakings,
> "As newborn babes, desire the sincere milk of the word, that ye may grow thereby:
> "If so be ye have tasted that the Lord is gracious."—1:23–2:3.

Peter relates the very salvation of the strangers scattered throughout those five Roman provinces of what is present-day Turkey with the incorruptibility of the seed of God's Word that has eternal characteristics: living, abiding and enduring. God's Word lives forever, and it abides forever, and it endures forever. When inspiration-preservation detractors say that that means God's Word is alive and present in perfect form only in Heaven, they miss the boat. Peter said that living, abiding, enduring Word, through the Gospel, brought about the salvation of people all over Asia Minor in the first century! Rather hard that would have been if the only location where that living, abiding, enduring Word could have been found had been Heaven.

Then, Peter addressed the passing grass of man's flesh and the withering flower of man's glory that stand in stark contrast to God's living, abiding, enduring Word. All the malice, guile, hypocrisy, envy, and evil speaking that accompany fleshly, human glory must be laid aside if any person is going to receive the Word of God and grow by it. Peter did not call these believers newborn babes, but exhorted them to desire the milk of God's Word as if they were. Who ever heard of a baby nursing at his mother's breast and suddenly complaining that the milk was not good? Babies do not express their opinions about breast milk, and believers should not opine about God's Word. They should receive it as it is, and when they do, they will taste the graciousness of the Lord.

With this background in Peter's first Epistle, consider II Peter 3:16–18 where he specifically called Paul's writings Scripture and said that "they that are unlearned and unstable wrest [them] unto their own destruction." In the next verse, he warned his readers not to follow those Scripture wresters "lest...being led away with the error of the wicked, [they] fall from [their] own stedfastness." Then, he commanded in the imperative mode for his followers to "grow in grace, and in the knowledge of our Lord and Saviour Jesus Christ," a command that can be obeyed only if people do not wrest the Scriptures to distortion but believe them in their perfection. In the name of higher criticism and Scripture readability, much Scripture wresting is occurring in the twenty-first century. All of it results in the hearers of such content being destroyed by their falling into error and their falling away from steadfast faith. None of these people grow in grace; hence, the multiversional crowd is characterized by deep intellect but shallow faith.

II and III John. These short canonical books mention the truth nine separate times. The last living apostle cited the truth in which he loved others, the truth governing God's love for man, the truth in which the believers in that assembly walked, the truth that was characteristic of Gaius, the truth to which believers may be fellow helpers, and the truth that gives believers good report. Indeed, the truth of which John wrote was the faith mentioned by Jude, the complete embodiment of revelation from the mouth of God.

It is this writer's opinion that II John was written to a local church, "the elect lady," and that III John was written to the pastor of that local church, namely Gaius. Within the church led by Gaius was a man named Demetrius who loved the truth and another individual called Diotrophes whose craving for preeminence resulted in his prating against the apostles with malicious words. John's use of the word "us" in III John 10 includes the other apostles who also received revelation from the resurrected Lord Jesus Christ. At the time that John wrote, all the other apostles were already dead, so John's reference that Diotrophes was using malicious words against them strongly indicates that he was teaching the false, antichrist doctrines mentioned in II John 7.

The concept of inspiration is found in II John 2 where John wrote, "For the truth's sake, which dwelleth in us." The very possibility, to say nothing of the reality, of truth dwelling within believers requires a source of that truth outside the believer. No man in himself has access to a private supply of truth. God is the wellspring from which the truth flows, and it was from God that the believers in John's day received inspired truth.

Preservation is found in John's confident words at the end of II John 2 where he said, "For the truth's sake, which...shall be with us for ever." God's preservational oversight of His truth occasioned the presence of inspired truth with believers as long as they lived.

Further strengthening the argument that John was defending inspired, preserved truth is the warning found in II John 7–11:

> *"For many deceivers are entered into the world, who confess not that Jesus Christ is come in the flesh. This is a deceiver and an antichrist.*
> *"Look to yourselves, that we lose not those things which we have wrought, but that we receive a full reward.*
> *"Whosoever transgresseth, and abideth not in the doctrine of Christ, hath not God. He that abideth in the doctrine of Christ, he hath both the Father and the Son.*
> *"If there come any unto you, and bring not this doctrine, receive him not into your house, neither bid him God speed:*
> *"For he that biddeth him God speed is partaker of his evil deeds."*

With both a solemn warning to be alert to Satan (the word antichrist) and a serious warning to be alert to oneself, John exposed the false doctrine that Bible changers were circulating even then. It is not far-fetched to assume that such false teachers as Diotrophes were publishing and peddling their articles to the unsuspecting and the undiscipled.

One can hardly believe that, while Jesus walked the Emmaus Road with Cleopas and his wife, He spent the time disproving inspiration and denying preservation. "He expounded unto them in all the scriptures the things concerning himself" (Luke 24:27) is a clear statement that He was not undermining the Scriptures but using them, not attacking the veracity of the record of Himself but avowing it. Those who have Emmaus Road "doctorates" embrace the fundamental doctrines of inspiration and preservation of the Scripture in the King James Bible for English-speaking peoples.

14

The Long and Short of It

The longest and shortest individual sections of Scripture are Psalms 119 and 117 respectively. Even though they have been referenced in other chapters, further mention is warranted.

Psalm 118:8 is beautifully placed between these two psalms and states the grand betterment and advantage of trusting God over putting confidence in men. Without a preserved Word from God, there is no way that man can trust Him. If, as the error-theorists presume, the Bible is riddled or even sprinkled with errors, it is impossible to trust God. Surrounded as Psalm 118:8 is by two psalms declaring the perfection of God's Word, it seems quite contextually obvious that God is saying that those who propose that God's Word is somehow flawed by the progression of time are the ones who are putting confidence in man.

Psalm 119, the Long of It. As the longest single portion of Scripture, Psalm 119 testifies abundantly of the eternality and preservation of Scripture. A brief overview of words employed by Ezra in the writing of this restoration psalm gives amazing insights.

Verb Expression. Verbs speak of action, and the action of God with regard to His Word is expressed in this Psalm through the use of verbs like *quicken* (vss. 25, 50, 93, 107, 149, 154, 156, 159); *stablish* (vs. 38); *hope* (vss. 49, 74, 81, 114, 116; 147); *settle* (vs. 89); *uphold* (vs. 116); *founded* (vs. 152) and *endure* (vs. 160). The writer, by inspiration, testifies of the power of the truth of God to quicken, that is, make alive. Could this be said of a man-tampered, man-tinkered, man-tainted book? This grand Word of God can give hope. Again, can that which is unreliable give hope? God is said to have established His Word to His servant, to have settled His Word forever, to have founded His Word forever, and to have ensured the endurance of His Word forever. Forever is a long time, and it seems that it includes the twenty-first century, in spite of the naysayers and gainsayers who insist that God's Word is neither established nor settled nor founded nor enduring!

Noun Expression. Nouns are the namers in the English language, telling either of a person, place, thing, or idea. Psalm 119 metaphorically calls the Word of God both a lamp and a light in verse 105. The same metaphor of light is found in verse 130. What kind of fool would use either a lamp or light that would not show the way? And how could God's Word be a lamp for our feet or a light for our path if His Word were full of mistakes? And in what manner could the entrance of God's Word give light to the simple if that very Word were inaccurate?

Perhaps the boldest noun used in the entire psalm is found in verse 142: "Thy law is the truth." Similar expressions are found just nine verses later: "All thy commandments are truth" (vs. 151); and nine verses later than that: "Thy word is true from the beginning" (vs. 160). No figurative statements, these! The words the truth are not the dynamic equivalent of what Jesus Christ called himself in John 14:6; rather, these words are the identical expression. If the truth in published form is faulty and full of failure, then so must be the Truth in personal form. How closely the fault-finding crowd stands by the precipice of blasphemy! How dangerously the fault-finding crowd wanders near the cliff of apostasy!

Adjective Expression. Adjectives, reserved in English for defining what kind or which one, also play a significant role in this psalm in describing the eternality and preservation of Scripture. Consider that God's commandments are called faithful (vss. 86, 138), a virtual lie if the commandments are inaccurate or tainted. God's precepts are esteemed as right (vs. 128) in all areas they address, an impossibility if they are wrongly expressed. The very next verse declares that God's testimonies are wonderful, another impossibility if those testimonies are diluted or contaminated by the ongoing progression of language and translation. Verses 137, 138 and 164 use the words *upright* and *righteous* to describe God's judgments and testimonies. That very righteousness ascribed to God's testimonies is said to be everlasting (vs. 144). These clear wordings can be said only in reference to perfect statements. God's "word is very pure" according to verse 140, another statement that can be correctly applied only to unflawed, perfect truth.

Significant Statements. Other statements in Psalm 119 would be moot and senseless without the immortality of God's truth in the Word of God. Verse sixty-four states, "The earth, O Lord, is full of thy mercy: teach me thy statutes." How, if the statutes that explain and enlarge upon God's mercy are flawed through the progression of language from generation to generation, could the whole earth be full of God's mercy? Again, the seventy-second verse exclaims, "The law of thy mouth is better unto me than thousands of gold and silver," a statement that could not possibly be true if the Law of God's mouth were quite possibly or even quite probably erroneous. And would not the eightieth verse that prays that the writer's heart would be sound in God's statutes be ridiculous if those very statutes were flawed and less than perfect?

Consider the bold declaration of verse ninety-two. Ezra stated that he would have perished in his affliction without the delights of God's law. Certainly no such delight could have been derived from a flawed, imperfect message. When the writer said he had taken God's "testimonies...as an heritage for ever (vs. 111), he implied the ongoing perfection of those testimonies. Without such a continuous perfection, no such heritage could have been claimed. And what kind of God would tread "down all them that err from [his] statutes" (vs. 118) if the statutes changed from generation to generation such that people would not know right from wrong? Such action would be the arbitrary injustice of a bullying god. However, if the statutes are unchanging—and they are—then all those who dare to tread down those statutes are accountable for them, and God is just to tread them down for such careless presumption.

Moreover, the psalmist's admission, "I am afraid of thy judgments" (v.120) is little more than the expression of a superstitious phobia if said judgments are subject to the whims of careless scribes and the degeneration of passing time. However, when one realizes and accepts that God's judgments are the immutable declarations of right and wrong for all mankind for all time, there is reason to have fear of them. One must ask why the Psalmist would weep and grieve over people's disregard of God's law (vss. 136, 158) if God's law were a fudged up collection of supposed truth.

Think of the complete senselessness of the verse 155 if Scripture is not perfectly preserved. This verse reads, "Salvation is far from the wicked: for they seek not thy statutes." The very substance of eternal salvation is linked to God's statutes, and without access to the Scripture, the wicked have no hope of being saved. This sounds much like the truth of Romans 10:17 that says, "So then faith cometh by hearing, and hearing by the word of God."

The psalmist wrote no fewer than eleven times of his love for God's Word. The fear cited earlier would be superstitious phobia; this love expressed in verses 47, 48, 97, 113, 119, 127, 140, 159, 163, 165 and 167 would be superstitious idolatry aside from the fact that God's Word is the totally perfect expression of the totally perfect God. Only with the flawlessness of God's Word can come God's approval upon His servant loving His Word.

Beyond thepPsalmist's love and resulting from it is his keeping of God's Word. Cited as a concept twenty-nine times (vss. 2, 4, 5, 8, 17, 22, 33, 34, 44, 55, 56, 57, 60, 63, 67, 69, 88, 100, 101, 106, 115, 129, 134, 136, 145, 146, 158, 167, and 168), Ezra testifies of his personal keeping of the law, command, testimony, precept, and judgment in twenty-four of those references! For a man such as Ezra who "was a ready scribe in the law of Moses" and "had prepared his heart to seek the law of the Lord, and to do it, and to teach in Israel statutes and judgments" (Ezra 7:6, 10) to place such emphasis upon keeping God's Word, there must be some strong reason for it. And strong reason there is. That strong reason is that God's Word is the infallible, immutable, incorruptible message of heaven to earth, and man's keeping of it yields "great reward" (Psalm 19:11).

Psalm 117, the Short of It. If the testimony of Psalm 119 is great, the testimony of Psalm 117 is greater! When God gave this little portion, He spoke of the two most important reasons for man in all the earth to praise Him: (1) the greatness of His merciful kindness toward us and (2) the endurance of His truth forever. Why would God not have used this pithy psalm to talk about His Creation, the most referred to miracle in all of Scripture? or the opening of the Red Sea? or the dynamic miracle workers and wonder-working prophets of bygone ages? or the amazing preservation of Israel? or the myriad answers to prayer from His people? or the unexplainable births like that of Isaac and Samuel? or a hundred other themes or subjects? Why? The simple answer is that without God's mercy to mankind and His truth enduring for every generation of mankind, none of these other things would be known or important.

In truth, the mercy of God toward man and His enduring truth have much in common. It is, first of all, through God's enduring truth from previous eras and historical times that man today comes into contact with the message and reality of God's merciful kindness. Without God's truth in preserved perfection, no person alive could ever lay claim to encountering or possessing the mercy of God! No message of salvation, of forgiveness of sin, of propitiation through faith in Christ's blood, of reconciliation through Christ's becoming sin for us, of peace through the blood of His cross, of deliverance from Hell, of eternity in Heaven, or of any of the other aspects of our eternal redemption could be credible if God's truth failed to be perfect at some historical point after its inspiration.

If, as the multiversion, dynamic equivalency crowd insists, the Scripture has mistakes, miscopyings and misunderstandings, where is the reliability of any concept of Christian living? of Christian discipleship? of Christian behavior? of Christian activity? of Christian responsibility?

Summed up in the shortest possible rendition, God commands all of mankind in every nation and among every people to praise Him for His mercy toward man and His truth for man. And that is the long and the short of it.

15

What's It Really All About?

In the final analysis, the entire anti-inspiration, antipreservation controversy is all about a worldwide effort to destroy the holiness and perfection of God's Word. Satan is behind this effort, around this effort and at the head of it. He hates God's Word. He employs any and all who, through ignorance or intention, will swallow his carnal intellectualism and worldly wisdom. In the English-speaking realm, his attack is against the King James Bible.

Interestingly, Satan's wrath has not been kindled against any of the copyrighted versions translated from the corrupted texts with their additions and deletions, their pollutions and dilutions, and their allowances and perversions. No other version is under attack at all. The newer versions simply die out of circulation for lack of interest and readership. No fear, however, because for every new version that is laid to rest with oratorical obsequies and honorable interments, several others rise to take its place.

Some of the people who are fighting on the anti-inspiration, antipreservation side are lost souls "who hold the truth in unrighteousness" and who are

> "filled with all unrighteousness, fornication, wickedness, covetousness, maliciousness; full of envy, murder, debate, deceit, malignity; whisperers,
> "Backbiters, haters of God, despiteful, proud, boasters, inventors of evil things, disobedient to parents,
> "Without understanding, covenantbreakers, without natural affection, implacable, unmerciful:

"Who knowing the judgment of God, that they which commit such things are worthy of death, not only do the same, but have pleasure in them that do them."—Romans 1:18, 29–32.

Who, more than a person who would question the veracity and authority of God in His Word, holds down the truth in the unrighteousness of his condemned soul? Who, more than one who dares to attack the beauty and glory of God's Word, is filled with all unrighteousness, wickedness, covetousness, maliciousness, envy, murder, debate, deceit, and malignity? Talk about malignity—these malign God by their treacherous and pernicious attacks against his precious revelation. Who, more than an individual who proposes that the Scripture is mistake filled and problem ridden, can be described as despiteful, proud, implacable or unmerciful? Who, more than these can be called haters of God, boasters, inventors of evil things, and covenant breakers? The answer is no one. No one has shown more spite, more pride, more implacability, and less mercy than he who ridicules the Bible as less than inspired, less than preserved, less than perfect, less than infallible. No one hates God more, boasts higher, invents more evil, and breaks a more valuable covenant than he who would stick out his stiff neck and call the Bible itself into question.

Others among the people who are on the anti-inspiration, anti-preservation team are saved souls, but they are ignorant of their salvation and all its glorious provisions. Perhaps they have failed to give "all diligence" and

"add to [their] faith virtue; and to virtue knowledge;
"And to knowledge temperance; and to temperance patience; and to patience godliness;
"And to godliness brotherly kindness; and to brotherly kindness charity."—II Peter 1:5–7.

Because of this, they are "barren" and "unfruitful in the knowledge of our Lord Jesus Christ" and "blind, and cannot see afar off, and [have] forgotten that [they were] purged from [their] old sins" (II Peter 1:8, 9).

Maybe they have failed to 'study to shew themselves approved unto God...workmen that need not to be ashamed, rightly dividing the word of truth.' Evidently, they have failed to "shun profane and vain babblings" (II Timothy 2:15, 16). Because of this, they have fallen prey to false teachers whose word doth "eat as doth a canker…Who concerning the truth have erred" and who "overthrow the faith of some" (vss. 17, 18).

Whether intentionally employed or ignorantly engaged, these people serve in the worldwide effort to eliminate the final authority of God among speakers of the English language by confusing the issues and muddying the waters of earnest contention for the faith. It is impossible to "earnestly contend for the faith which was once delivered unto the saints" (Jude 3) while one undermines the very vehicle that communicates that faith.

It really is all about Satan's millennia-long hatred of the truth and his time-tested attack methods of adding to what God said, taking away from what God said, and thus making what God said what the Devil said. A poet of the past wrote, "Hammer away ye rebel bands. Your hammers break; God's anvil stands."

We who love the Scriptures and believe it to be inspired and preserved for the English-speaking world in the venerable, four-hundred-year-old King James Bible are among the chosen souls of all time who have earnestly contended for the faith. Those who love the blessed Word of God and accept without question its perfect inspiration and inerrant preservation for the English-speaking millions in the God-honoring, Christ-exalting, Holy-Spirit-agreeing, soul-saving, heart-cleansing, life-changing, revival-spawning, church-building, missionary-sending King James Scripture are counted with those of all previous generations who have earnestly contended for the faith.

Change the Bible, or let the Bible change you. That's what it's really all about.

patrician 1. (Rom. Antiq.) Of or pertaining to the Roman patres (fathers) or senators, or patricians. 2. Of, pertaining to, or appropriate to, a person of high birth; noble; not plebian.

ex nihilo out of nothing; from nothing.

autographa "The original manuscript (the original parchment the author physically wrote on)"—Wikipedia (Biblical Manuscript)

hermeneutical interpreting; explaining; unfolding the signification; as hermeneutic theology, the art of expounding the Scriptures.

veracity 1.Habitual observance of truth, or habitual truth; as a man of veracity. His veracity is not called in question. The question of the court is, whether you know the witness to be a man of veracity. We rely on history, when we have confidence in the veracity and industry of the historian. 2. Invariable expression of truth; as the veracity of our senses.

aver To affirm with confidence; to declare in a positive or peremptory manner, as in confidence of asserting the truth.

*magnum opus a great work, especially the chief work of a writer or artist.

exactitude Exactness. [Little used.]

*intertestamental of or pertaining to the period between the close of the Old Testament and the beginning of the New Testament.

*remonstrate 1. to say or plead in protest, objection or disapproval. 2. Obsolete, to show

egregious 1. Eminent; remarkable; extraordinary; distinguished; as egregious exploits; an egregious prince. But in this sense it is seldom applied to persons. 2. In a bad sense, great; extraordinary; remarkable; enormous; as an egregious mistake; egregious contempt. In this sense it is often applied to persons; as an egregious rascal; an egregious murderer.

vernal 1. Belonging to the spring; appearing in spring; as vernal bloom. 2. Belonging to youth, the spring of life.

supernal Relating to things above; celestial; heavenly; as supernal grace. Not by the sufferings of supernal pow'r.

*infinitude 1. infinity: divine infinitude. 2. an infinite extent, amount or number.

Stygian 1. Sharp; bitter; corrosive; abounding with acrimony. 2. Figuratively, sharpness or severity of temper; bitterness of expression proceeding from anger, ill-nature or petulance.

pernicious 1. Destructive; having the quality of killing, destroying or injuring; very injurious or mischievous. Food, drink or air may be pernicious to life or health. 2. Destructive; tending to injure or destroy. Evil examples are pernicious to morals. Intemperance is a pernicious vice. 3. [L. pernix.] Quick. [Not used.]

mendacious Lying; false. [Little used.]

*lexicography 1. the writing, editing or compiling of dictionaries. 2. the principles and procedures involved in writing, editing or compiling dictionaries.

legerdemain Slight of hand; a deceptive performance which depends on dexterity of hand; a trick performed with such art and adroitness, that the manner or art eludes observation. The word is sometimes used adjectively; as a legerdemain trick.

efficacious Effectual; productive of effects; producing the effect intended; having power adequate to the purpose intended; powerful; as an efficacious remedy for disease.

*ubiquitous Existing or being everywhere, especially at the same time; omnipresent: *ubiquitous fog; ubiquitous little ants.*

pontificating "speaking or behaving in a pompous or dogmatic manner"—Colliers English Dictionary

*pejoration 1. depreciation; a lessening in worth, quality, etc. 2. *Historical Linguistics.* semantic change in a word to a lower, less approved, or less respectable meaning. Compare melioration def. 1

minutiae The smaller particulars.

licentious 1. Using license; indulging freedom to excess; unrestrained by law or morality; loose; dissolute; as a licentious man. 2.

166

Exceeding the limits of law or propriety; wanton; unrestrained; as licentious desires. Licentious thoughts precede licentious conduct.

erudite Instructed; taught; learned.

exegetical Explanatory; tending to unfold or illustrate; expository.

calumnious Slanderous; bearing or implying calumny; injurious to reputation.

Gordian knot Gordian knot, in antiquity, a knot in the leather or harness of Gordius, a king of Phrygia, so very intricate that there was no finding where it began or ended. An oracle declared that he who should untie this knot should be master of Asia. Alexander, fearing that his inability to untie it should prove an ill augury, cut it asunder with his sword. Hence, in modern language, a Gordian knot is an inextricable difficulty; and to cut the Gordian knot is to remove a difficulty by bold or unusual measures.

nebulous 1. Cloudy; hazy. 2. Resembling a small cloud or collection of vapors.

efficacious Effectual; productive of effects; producing the effect intended; having power adequate to the purpose intended; powerful; as an efficacious remedy for disease.

All definitions unless otherwise noted came from the *1828 Webster's Dictionary*.

Definitions notated with * came from *Dictionary.com*.

Pontificating came from *Colliers English Dictionary*.

Autographa came from Wikipedia (Biblical Manuscript).

For a complete list of available
books, please go to
swordofthelord.com.